SERIAL KILLERS

101 QUESTIONS TRUE CRIME FANS ASK

JONI JOHNSTON, Psy.D.

WILDBLUE
PRESS
WildBluePress.com

SERIAL KILLERS published by:
WILDBLUE PRESS
P.O. Box 102440
Denver, Colorado 80250

ISBN 978-1-952225-51-2 Trade Paperback
ISBN 978-1-52225-50-5 eBook

Interior Formatting/Book Cover Design by Elijah Toten
www.totencreative.com

SERIAL KILLERS

Table of Contents

Serial Killers: 101 Questions True Crime Fans Ask

I've thought about my fascination with serial killers a lot, especially given my chosen profession. Why *did* I become a forensic psychologist and private investigator? What is it about the criminal mind that is so compelling?

There's a back story to this plot. While I didn't know it when I got hooked at age fourteen after reading Vincent Bugliosi's book, *Helter Skelter*, about Charles Manson and his "family" while on a vacation with my own, I am a legacy of true crime lovers. My mom was a diehard whodunit aficionado. *Columbo*, *Hawaii Five-0*, *Dragnet*; whenever these shows were on TV, she was parked in front of it. On one vacation, we even drove out of the way to see the Clutter farm, where the tragic family murder featured in Truman Capote's classic *In Cold Blood* took place. Maybe I inherited my interest from her.

Maybe it's my personality. I've always rooted for the underdog, which may have inspired my interest in victim's rights and child-abuse prevention. I've always loved scary movies; perhaps that's a link to my attraction to the dark side of human nature. There have been times when I've felt trapped by my empathy. Could this have fueled my curiosity about psychopaths, people who feel free to do whatever they want without any concern for others?

I'm still not sure I have the personal answer to those questions. But I know I'm not alone. If you are reading this book, I assume that you, too, are interested in true crime. Hundreds of thousands of people are. Which, by the way, is nothing new. Serial killers and other bad guys have attracted attention since the rise of mass-circulation newspapers in the early nineteenth century. The reasons why are complicated.

First of all, it's hard to wrap our minds around a seemingly normal human being—someone who is able to blend in and fool everyone—who is secretly boiling a victim's head or having sex with a corpse. The discrepancy between how a serial killer appears and how they really are is both horrifying and compelling; we ask, how can a person capable of such atrocities be hiding in plain sight?

Then there's the "better the devil you know" theory. While it can be scary to learn about the horrible things people do—and have done—it can be empowering to understand the motivations, emotions and actions of dangerous people. Maybe it can help us figure out what people and situations to avoid, and how to spot, and report, something that doesn't seem right. As a crime writer, I've often been amazed at the safety tips that my true-crime readers share. And, while no one thinks interfering in a police investigation is a good idea, everyday citizens who've spoken up have prevented suicides, solved missing-persons cases, and, by providing useful information to law enforcement, even solved murders.

There's also the true-crime-as-a-catharsis theory. Just as horror movies allow us to experience fear and excitement from a distance, reading about convicted serial killers can be a safe and controlled way to experience the endorphin and adrenaline rush of fear without ever being in harm's way. In essence, it's cathartic; we experience uncomfortable emotions in a controlled way, knowing there will be justice in the end. In some ways, it's similar to our need to look at car accidents, train wrecks, or natural disasters; we might feel guilty about looking, but it sure is hard to look away.

The media may also have something to do with it. Contrary to some, I don't think the media glorifies serial killers. I do think, however, they often sensationalize them in order to tell a good story. Any good fiction writer knows that, unless your readers can sympathize with the "bad guy," they will not continue reading. There are lots of ways writers do this—provide an understanding of why they do what they do, show the villain doing something nice early on, imply that they regret something from the past, and so forth. Applying these tactics to real-life villains, though, can have unfortunate side effects; callous serial killers who tortured innocent victims can come across as misunderstood and attractive-but-evil geniuses.

Some, or all, of these theories might ring true to you. I might have been a lifelong crime junkie rather than a forensic psychologist and private investigator if it wasn't for two things. One, growing up with a seriously mentally ill family member left me with a hunger to understand the human mind, all the ways it works and all the ways it doesn't. And, when I was a senior in high school, Ted Bundy broke out of a Colorado jail and wound up murdering young sorority girls at the Chi Omega sorority house at Florida State University. I was a high school senior, the campus was an hour and a half from my home, and some of the victims looked a lot like me. My interest in human nature took a dark turn into the criminal mind.

My first official foray into forensic psychology began as soon as I finished graduate school. My first job was working with victims of abuse or neglect, where I got an up-close-and-personal look at the impact of trauma on children. We were all too young to see such pain—maybe we *all* are, no matter how old—but it took its toll. We coped by going out together and getting drunk every few months to blow off steam. There were times when I was filled with rage; I once commented that, if the electric chair were still in vogue, I would volunteer to flip the switch.

For the most part, the abuser was in the family. I saw mothers call their children liars just to keep a man around. I heard perpetrators deny the evidence sitting right in front of them or blame it on the most innocent victim; I once heard a sex offender comment on the provocativeness of his 4-year-old victim. But I also saw women who were blindsided by a child's abuse, who responded with full and loving support and a desire for justice. I also saw fathers who were working hard to break the violent, and often multigenerational, legacy of their own fathers. I saw most children on the path to recovery. And I saw a few who scared me.

Later in my career, I worked in a maximum-security prison, among inmates for whom the boundaries between victim and perpetrator were often blurred. Many of these men and women had experienced trauma they didn't even recognize; in fact, one of the first things I learned during an interview was to ask about specific experiences rather than about general abuse because so many described their childhood as normal. And they believed it.

Think that I'm some bleeding-heart idealist who thinks that abuse is an excuse for the behaviors of the perpetrators in this book? Let me reassure you. By the time you or I are introduced to any one of these adults—and likely long before that—any chance of rehabilitating them is long gone. Not only are the majority of adults who engage in violent predatory behavior not likely to change, they don't want to. It takes a certain kind of irreparable psyche to cold-bloodedly carry out the murder of someone just to get an orgasm, to feel a different kind of thrill or to make a buck. The best the rest of us can do is go about our lives as safely as possible, learn the warning signs of a dangerous personality and, if we see something that's odd or worrisome in them, speak up.

But it is also true that no one is born a serial killer. If we continue to think of serial killers as monsters instead of adults who consciously decide to hurt other people and who were once babies and toddlers who didn't, we're never going to understand why a third of abused children become abusers themselves while the vast majority don't. We'll never learn how to tell the difference between a teen who doesn't want to be controlled (which is normal) and an adolescent who constantly tries to control others (which is not). Or even how some psychopathic adults use their personalities to become successful businessmen and businesswomen while others spend their lives committing murder and mayhem. There are many steps along the path to becoming a serial killer and some of them include opportunities for intervention before it's too late. We need to be able to recognize every step.

So, let's get started. As the title suggests, this book is organized by questions, many of which I received from readers of my *Psychology Today* blog, viewers of my YouTube channel, and listeners of my radio show/ podcast. I have also added case studies to support many of the questions, trying to focus on more recent cases and/ or international cases that may not be as familiar as those spotlighted in the media.

At times, I have also done the reverse: I've started out with a certain case and then used it to ask a deeper question. So, for example, in a recent case about a teen serial killer, I tell you about the case and then talk about (and encourage you to think about) the unique challenges and dilemmas we have in dealing with these young but frightening perpetrators.

As interesting as these cases are, let's never forget that they involve real people's lives.

Part 1: Who are they? Statistics, Demographics and Definitions.

Since 1900, there have been 3,000 identified American serial killers responsible for close to 10,000 deaths.

1. What Is a Serial Killer? It depends on who you ask and how you define it. The term didn't even exist until the 1970s; before then, they were referred to as "mass murderers. Before *that*, you'd have to search for terms like "convicted of three murders" or "shot four people" and then determine whether it was a mass murder or serial killing. It's possible that there were just as many serial killers in the 1950s as the 1970s, but because we didn't have that term, we didn't recognize them.

But in the 1990s, the powers that be decided it was time to get serious about just who a serial killer really was. In 1998, the U.S. Congress defined a serial killer as *three or more* victims, killed over time with common characteristics to suggest that the same offender committed the murders. Some researchers still argue that, because a serial killer is such a rarity, we should make sure their body count reflects this and go for the higher number. Since 2005, though, the FBI has redefined a serial killer as a person who has killed *two or more* individuals on two separate occasions. Not only did they loosen up their triple-homicide requirement, they also did away with the psychological "cooling off" period that is the hallmark of sexual serial murders.

What we're left with is a person who kills two or more people at different times. That's a pretty broad definition and, in some ways, doesn't help us much. Kelly Cochran, who, along with her husband, killed her lover and bumped off her spouse, doesn't have much in common with Samuel Little, the sexual serial killer who confessed to murdering ninety-three vulnerable women.

The reason the definition is so broad is that the FBI wanted to give itself a lot of leeway to help local law enforcement with serial crimes, so they narrowed the body-count requirement from three to two. In some ways, it makes sense to use two as a marker. The vast majority of murderers kill only one person, so while there are many differences among serial murders, the fact that they have killed more than one person puts them in a unique category, one that's all the more unique given the fact that these murders were planned and not the tragic result of a fight or argument. On the other hand, the narrower definition definitely lets in murderers who have killed two people at different times who don't fit our common understanding of serial murder. So, the debate continues.

Who Invented the Term "Serial Killer?"

According to most sources, the term "serial killer" was invented when FBI profiler Robert Ressler was a lecturer at a British police academy. He got the idea for it in 1974 after he noticed a series of reoccurring rapes, murders, arsons and robberies that were carried out by the same perpetrators and seemed to escalate over time. Why, he wondered, did these repeat offenders keep doing the same thing over and over, often in more violent ways and with shorter times in between crimes?

Just like the popular "serial adventure" shows he used to watch as a boy at Saturday matinees during the 1930s and 1940s, which had season-long storylines with tension-building episodes that always left the audience wanting more, Ressler thought that perhaps repeat killers felt unsatisfied after each murder because it never lived up to the fantasy they imagined. As a result, tension built up and s/he eventually felt a need to commit murder again in the hope of, this time, attaining perfection. Unlike the eventual resolution to the Saturday morning cliffhangers as the season ended, though, the serial murders didn't typically end until the offender was killed or captured.

Undoubtedly, Ressler was *one* of the first to use the term "serial killer." But not everyone thinks he was *the* first. Crime historian Harold Schechter came across what he believes to be the first use of the term "serial killer" dating back to 1930s Germany, when the director of the Berlin Criminal Police, Ernst August Ferdinand Gennat, used the term "serienmorder" (or, in English, serial killers) in the 1933 book *The Monster of Dusseldorf.*

2. What Is the Typical Demographic Profile of a Serial Killer? In the heyday of serial killers (the 1970s and 1980s), the "typical" profile of a serial murderer was a single, white male; a loner, misfit, underemployed, in his twenties or thirties, who murders after his longstanding deviant sexual fantasies no longer satisfy him and a stressful life event finally propels him into action.

Times have changed. Today, only 12.5 percent (one-eighth) of American serial killers fit this profile. Men still dominate, committing 85 to 90 percent of serial murders. Caucasian serial killers (52 percent) still edge out black serial killers (40 percent), with other races barely represented; Hispanics come in a distant third at around 7 percent. Native Americans and Asians barely show up at 1 percent or less.

And not all—or even most—serial killers are driven by sex. Yes, we still have sexually motivated serial killers and they still dominate media coverage. But we also have serial killers who murder because it's easier than divorce, or out of revenge or because it's fun. And, for many serial killers, control is much more of a turn-on than sex.

Culture's Killers

Ever wonder if a serial killer from the U.S. would still be a serial killer if he were raised in another country—or vice versa? A psychopath in the U.S. would probably not be a good guy anywhere else. But we also know that the culture in which they live; they might still hurt people, but how or who or why might be different. Throughout time, a country's social problems and cultural values and beliefs has influenced the choices a serial killer makes in terms of the victim he chooses, the way he lures his victims, and the manner in which he kills.

Consider the hundreds of babies who died of abuse and neglect on "baby farms" at the turn of the twentieth century. Before adoption or abortion were legal in the U.S., the U.K. and Australia, desperate single mothers turned their infants over to alleged childcare providers, paying them to either find a home for their baby or take care of it until they return. Instead of keeping their promise, some women pocketed the money and either starved the infants to death or murdered them. Amelia Dyer is perhaps the most infamous serial-killing baby farmer; while she was convicted of murdering six infants in 1896, she may have killed as many as four hundred.

A more recent example of culture and serial killers colliding is Indian serial killer Mohan Kumar, who was recently tried and convicted for his twentieth victim. Kumar had a particularly devious (and odious) method or recruiting and dispatching victims. He would take his time courting his victims, getting acquainted with them and proposing marriage, and then persuading them to consummate their relationship at a nearby hotel.

Under a pretext, the next day he would ask them to leave their jewelry in the hotel room and give them a "contraceptive"—after all, no one wanted the shame of an unwanted pregnancy. The pill was actually cyanide, which resulted in a gruesome and painful death. (Later you will meet his female counterpart, K.D. Kempamma, aka Cyanide Mallika, who also used cyanide but had a very different way of luring her victims). It's hard to imagine a serial killer using the similar modus operandi in the U.S., where poison is rarely used and there is neither the same degree of societal pressure for single women to get married or the severe stigma of premarital sex or single motherhood.

3. How Can You Tell Who's a Serial Killer? It's pretty damn hard, if not impossible. How many times have we heard of a serial killer being arrested and the first response of neighbors, friends, and family members was "He was just the nicest guy?" There are serial killers who have fooled smart judges, savvy police officers, skilled investigators, and skeptical parole boards. The bottom line is that there are some serial killers who you or I would never suspect even if they were operating right under our noses.

However, there are other serial killers who are bad news in every aspect of their lives. They are controlling and manipulative. They hit their kids or their partners. They act out deviant behaviors in the bedroom such as nonconsensual bondage, "pretend" strangling, or by being unusually rough with a reluctant or unwilling partner. They disappear and lie about where they've been. They exhibit a general lack of empathy in how they treat others. They commit other petty crimes: fraud, theft, drug possession. Rarely, a serial killer will give more obvious clues: an obsession with certain homicide or abduction cases; telling weird jokes about rape or murder; bragging about his ability to get away with murder; leaving an unknown woman's clothing or jewelry around. Serial killer or not, staying in a relationship with someone like this is likely to psychologically kill you even if the person isn't planning to physically finish you off.

Serial Killers: How Do We Know It's the Same Guy?

The criminal career of Joseph James DeAngelo shows just how hard it can be to link crimes to the same offender. Between 1974 and 1975, a prolific prowler, burglar, and voyeur plagued the town of Visalia, California. Unlike most burglars, the "Visalia Ransacker" didn't target big-ticket items; he would often steal small, often personal trinkets. He stole one victim's driver's license; he snatched a male victim's baseball cap. He often stole one earring and left the other one.

He also seemed to get pleasure out of wreaking havoc inside the victim's home, tossing the contents of drawers all over the room, pushing over bookshelves, or pouring wine or spraying shaving cream on the furniture and carpet. These crimes seemed to have a sexual component, as evidenced by his collecting and posing female undergarments and at times leaving hand lotion and a porn magazine at the crime scene. Based on these unique and consistent aspects of the crimes, police estimated DeAngelo committed up to one hundred and twenty offenses. Suddenly, in December 1975, the crimes stopped.

However, on June 18, 1976, another predator made his debut, over three hours north of Visalia and with a different agenda. This time, he focused on sexual assault. Over the next two years, he was linked to thirty-eight attacks between Sacramento and Stockton, starting out attacking women in their homes and then targeting couples. He was dubbed the East Area Rapist because he began his sexual assaults on the east side of Sacramento county. Like the Visalia Ransacker, this perpetrator exhibited a number of distinct (although different from the Ransacker) behaviors during his crimes, such as spending several hours in the homes (and, at times eating their food). When he targeted couples, he would tie up the man and balance dishes on his back, warning him that, if he heard a dish fall or break, he would kill everyone in the house.

Between 1978 and 1986, the Golden State Killer emerged. Unlike the Visalia Ransacker and the East Area Rapist, this predator murdered his victims and left a path of destruction from Orange County to Sacramento. DNA was left at some of the crime scenes but there was no match in available databases. In 2001, DNA from Golden State murders and East Area rapes were linked, indicating they were committed by the same perpetrator. But police had no suspects.

In 2018, Joseph James DeAngelo was arrested with the help of genetic genealogy. DNA from some of the crime scenes were uploaded onto a genealogy website and researchers put together a family tree, systematically eliminating suspects based on age and location until they narrowed it down to Mr. DeAngelo. Police officers then tailed him, looking for an opportunity to collect his DNA on a discarded piece of trash. They finally succeeded and, when they compared it to that left at some of the crime scenes, it was a match. They were astonished to learn that DeAngelo was not only the Golden State Killer and East Area rapist; he was also the Visalia Ransacker. The same perpetrator had operated using three distinct modus operandi (ways of committing his offenses) and unique signatures (rituals that gave him psychological satisfaction).

4. What Are the Different Types of Male Serial Killers?
There have been a number of ways researchers and law enforcement have tried to slice and dice serial killers in order to understand and capture them. One of the first, based on FBI interviews with thirty-six incarcerated serial killers between 1976 and 1979, was to separate them into broad categories of organized versus disorganized offenders. The thinking back then was that some serial killers were methodical and planned their crimes, as evidenced by behaviors such as picking out and stalking a particular victim, bringing a weapon with them, and carefully cleaning up afterward. These organized killers carefully controlled their crime scenes and left little evidence when they left. (TV serial killer Dexter would be an example).

Disorganized serial killers, on the other hand, were more likely to act spontaneously. Unlike the charm often used by organized killers to lure their victims, disorganized killers tended to disarm them with surprise and violence. These killers were more likely to choose a victim based on opportunity (a young person walking alone at night, for example), kill with their hands or a weapon found at the scene (such as a rock or piece of clothing) and make no attempt to hide the body. An FBI investigative analysis of the never-captured "Jack the Ripper," for instance, concluded that this perpetrator was a disorganized killer, given he chose his victims based on opportunity, overtook them in a blitz attack, and left them just like he killed them.

If this is how he commits his crimes, the thinking at the time went, this is probably how he lives his life. So, they hypothesized, an organized serial killer was likely to be smart, socially skilled, cunning, and controlled. The disorganized killer, on the other hand, was either a marginally functioning member of society (low intelligence, socially awkward, low job or educational status) or someone who was young, under the influence of drugs or alcohol or suffering a serious mental illness.

However, recent research has called into question the usefulness of these two categories, suggesting that most serial murders are organized (to a greater or lesser degree). It also found that many of the organized crime scenes also have some elements of disorganization. So, for example, you might have a serial killer who targets a specific victim and brings a weapon with him (suggesting an organized offender) who leaves the weapon behind and makes no attempt hide the body (suggesting disorganization). In other words, there's so much crime-scene overlap between "organized" and "disorganized" behaviors that attempting to separate serial killers based on such criteria may not be particularly useful. (A third category of "mixed" was added, but what good does that do?)

There have also been attempts to separate serial killers by their motives. The FBI includes the following motivations in their analysis of serial murderers:

- **Anger** is a motivation in which an offender displays rage or hostility toward a certain subgroup of the population or with society as a whole. One example is Todd Kolhepp, who murdered seven people between 2003 and 2016. He allegedly shot four of his victims after one of them teased him, was known for making verbal threats, and was once described by a neighbor as a "devil on a chain." According to his mother, Todd Kolhepp had been angry since he was old enough to express it and, even as a child, had a pattern of wrecking classmates' school projects, hurting animals, and as a teenager, raping a 14-year-old neighbor.
- **Criminal enterprise** is a motivation in which the offender gets money or gains status by committing murder that is related to drugs, gangs, or organized crime. Some serial killer experts argue that contract killers should be excluded because they are essentially performing a job, not living out a fantasy when they kill. That seems like a somewhat arbitrary distinction for me. There have been plenty of serial killers who bumped off spouses or family members for insurance money; the only fantasy they were entertaining at the time of their murders was how they were going to spend the money. There are also a lot of other jobs beside professional murderer that one could choose to make a living. So, arguably, there must be *some* psychological payoff for the professional hitman.

  In support of my argument is Richard Kuklinski, also known as "the Iceman." Over a span of thirty years (ending in 1988, when he was convicted of two murders), he claimed to have killed over two hundred people for various crime families. In his spare time, he also bumped off people for free, especially strangers who irritated or annoyed him.

• **Financial gain** is a motivation in which the offender directly benefits financially from killing, usually through an insurance payout or inheritance. (More rarely, the perpetrator kills to avoid paying wages or paying back debts). In July 2020, for instance, Indian serial killer Devender Sharma confessed to murdering fifty taxi drivers between 2002 and 2004 in order to sell the cars for profit. He and his accomplices also targeted truck drivers carrying LPG gas cylinders; they would lure the driver into a fake gas station, kill the driver, and sell off the taxi cabs. Never one to take the law-abiding path when a criminal one was available, his previous "job" was as an Ayurvedic practitioner in a scheme involving at least one hundred and twenty-five illegal kidney transplants.

• **Ideology** is a motivation to kill so that "higher" goals and ideas of a specific individual or group will be realized. This could include organized terrorist groups or one or more individuals who attack a specific racial, gender, or ethnic group. Serial bomber Ted Kaczynski would be one example; between 1978 and 1995, he killed three people and injured twenty-three others with mailed or hand-delivered bombs, all in the name of sabotaging modern technology. John Paul Franklin, who was fanatical about racial purity, would be another example. Between 1977 and 1980, he killed twelve young black males who had white girlfriends. And don't overlook dastardly duo Wolfgang Abel and Marco Furlan. Influenced by Nazi philosophy, their absolute disdain for, and desire to destroy, people whom they regarded as the dregs of society—homosexuals, sex workers, and drug addicts—led to the murders of twenty-seven people between 1977 and 1984 (although they were only convicted of ten).

• **Power/thrill** is a motivation in which the offender gets off on the power and excitement he feels when murdering his victims. Between May 2005 and August 2006, Dale Shawn Hauser and Samuel John Dieteman teamed up for a series of night-time drive-by shootings that left eight random people dead and eighteen more wounded in Phoenix, Arizona. The victims were either walking or riding a bicycle when they were gunned down; a horse and several dogs were also shot. The two would ride around at night in Hauser's car with a duffel bag containing guns in the back seat. When they spotted a potential victim, they would slow down, sometimes circling back to pass the person again. Then, they would strike. Wire taps before the two were arrested captured them reliving the murders and making fun of the victims; the sole motive seemed to be the thrill they received trolling around and executing complete strangers.

• **Psychosis** is a motivator when an offender suffers from a severe mental illness that induces him to kill, typically through auditory and/or visual hallucinations, and paranoid, grandiose, or bizarre delusions. While some forensic psychologists have been bamboozled into thinking that a bizarre or unusually violent crime scene was evidence of psychosis, this is not the case. In fact, true visionary serial killers are exceedingly rare. The most infamous in the United States is the previously mentioned Herbert Mullin, whose delusional beliefs caused him to sacrifice people to avoid an earthquake. Raman Raghav, an Indian serial killer active between 1965 and 1966, and again in 1968, confessed to forty-one murders of random men, women, and children (even a few babies). Victims were typically bludgeoned to death with an iron bar while they slept. He was evaluated by three psychiatrists after his arrest and diagnosed with chronic paranoid schizophrenia; he eventually died in a psychiatric institution in 1987. During his interrogation and later psychiatric evaluations, he expressed a number of bizarre beliefs: there were two distinct worlds, including one called Kanoon; he was an instrument of God, who sometimes told him to kill; other people were trying to get him to engage in gay sex, which would turn him into a woman, etc. However, while he genuinely seemed to suffer from a psychotic illness, it's not clear that he was insane; he hid his murder weapon, he used several aliases, and, when he was arrested, he refused to give a confession until several of his demands (including a dinner of chicken curry) were met. He was also able to lead the investigators on a detailed tour of his murders.

• **Sex** is a motivation when murder is driven by the sexual needs/desires of the offender, regardless of whether there is overt sexual contact during the commission of the crime. This motivation is what most of us think of when we think of a serial killer although sex is not actually the number-one motive of most serial killers; enjoyment is. In other words, the majority of serial killers murder because it brings them pleasure but sex is only one kind. Examples of sexually-motivated serial murderers include Gary Ridgway (1982-98; convicted of forty-nine sex-worker murders), Jerry Brudos (murdered at least four women between January 1968 and April 1969), and recently convicted Joseph James DeAngelo (killed at least thirteen women in California during the 1970s and 1980s).

One of the biggest challenges—and frustrations—for those of us who study serial killers is the fact that they (like the rest of humankind) don't fit neatly into little boxes. It's not uncommon for serial killers to have multiple motives; revenge against a society who they believe has mistreated them, robbing (financial) a victim after raping and torturing them (power/thrill), etc. And let's not forget that the crime scenes of some serial killers are so gruesome or bizarre that it's easy to jump to the conclusion that mental illness played a role (although, in reality, it rarely does).

What Was the *Real* Motive?

The Pakistani serial killer, Javed Iqbal, confessed to the rape, torture, and murder of one hundred young boys, ranging in age from six to sixteen, during a six-month period in 1999. Iqbal's initial claim was that his heinous acts were in retaliation for police brutality after they had arrested him for sodomizing children between 1985 and 1990; that's pretty ironic given that he was complaining about their response to *his* sadism. He then produced a 32-page diary that contained detailed descriptions of his deeds along with the names, ages, and pictures of his victims.

However, he later claimed it was an elaborate attempt to teach poor Pakistani parents a perverted lesson about what happens when they neglect their children. I think we can all safely assume that neither of his acclaimed explanations were accurate; given the gruesome details in his diary of what he did to his victims, it is clear that he got personal and sexual satisfaction from his crimes.

His crimes were so horrific that, during his trial, he was sentenced to be strangled one hundred times, his body cut into one hundred pieces, and the rest dissolved in acid. However, before his sentence was carried out, he was found dead in his prison cell in 2001. His death was officially listed as a suicide although some prison officials believe he met with a little vigilante justice from other inmates.

5. How Are Serial Killers Different Than Mass Murderers? Unlike serial murder, a mass murder is a one-time event that involves the killing of four or more people (excluding the perpetrator) with no cooling-off period between the murders. Victims may be either randomly selected (for example, the 2017 shooting of country music festival attendees by Stephen Paddock, resulting in fifty-eight deaths) or targeted for a specific reason (such as the Columbine High School shooting of students). Victims can include family members, coworkers, students, or random strangers.

The individual motives for mass murder vary greatly. A common motivation for mass murder is retaliation or revenge (on specific individuals or society in general) but other motivations are possible, including terrorism, a perverse quest for attention/fame or a distorted sense of loyalty (such as the financially failing father who decides to take out his entire family and then himself to spare them the shame of ruin). While we don't often think of it, there can even be a financial angle to mass murder; consider the bank robber who shoots several employees during a robbery to eliminate eyewitnesses.

Are Mass Shootings Contagious?

Certainly not in the way COVID-19 is. Nor does a mass shooting inspire a well-adjusted person to suddenly pick up a gun and start shooting. But, if you take an angry, severely depressed and desperate individual and expose him to a highly publicized mass or school shooting, it *could* tip him over the edge.

In 2014 and 2015, Arizona researchers analyzed a conglomeration of mass and school shooting data between 1998 and 2013 to see if they could spot any patterns or trends. What they found was that mass shootings tended to occur in clusters, with one shooting leading to others *in the two weeks after the initial event*. The "copycat" perpetrators tended to be vulnerable individuals who were suicidal and already considering violence; the well-publicized mass shooting simply gave them an easy act to follow.

6. What Are Spree Killers? Spree killers are in a gray area; they tend to fall in between our definition of serial killer and mass murderer. Because of this, we don't quite know what to do with them. On the one hand, we have our serial killers, who kill at least two people in distinct and separate events. On the other hand, we have our mass murderer, who kills at least four people in one basic locale (even if this involves going to different offices or several buildings in a block) in a short, defined time frame.

But what about a killer who kills at least three people in several different locations in a fairly short time period (typically less than week), much shorter than the typical "cooling off" period associated with some serial killers but a significantly longer one than for a mass murder? Or what if the murders appear to arise from a key participating event as opposed to the general need to get revenge on society (often seen in mass murder) or to satisfy some psychological thrill (often seen in serial killers)? Before 2005, these would be classified as spree killers, i.e., killers who fall somewhere in between mass murderers and serial killers.

For example, in 2017, Kori Ali Muhammed was wanted in connection with the shooting death of a motel employee at a Motel 6 in Fresno, California, a murder he later confessed to committing. His response to police pursuit was, in his own words, to decide he wasn't "going down" because he killed someone who "disrespected" him and decided to "kill as many white men as possible" before he was caught. Over the next few hours, he killed three of them at different locations—one sitting inside a utility truck, one walking home from a food pantry, and one waiting for a bus—before he was arrested.

A more recent example is that of Nova Scotian Gabriel Wortman, who, in April 2020 and after a domestic dispute, killed twenty-two people over a 13-hour period. He started his spree by seriously injuring his girlfriend, then targeted neighbors and acquaintances with whom he had had disputes over the past several years. He moved on to complete strangers before eventually being killed by police.

Some research suggests that there is little psychological distinction between a serial killer and a spree killer. Since the FBI symposium in 2005, this term has fallen out of vogue and formerly identified spree killers are now categorized as serial killers. There may be times, though, when it might be critical to identify a person who is targeting multiple people at different locations for a specific reason; if done early enough, it would be possible to predict his next move and warn potential victims. Between May 20 and June 4, 2018, Dwight Lamon Jones murdered six people, including a forensic psychologist, forensic psychiatrist, two paralegals, and a counselor. The motive appeared to be revenge, as all of the victims had played a role in his bitter 2009 divorce. If someone had recognized the common link between his first few victims, the others might have been spared.

Where Do Canadian Teen Killers Kam McLeod and Bryer Schmegelsky Fit In?

These two recent high-school graduates left their Vancouver Island home on July 12, 2019, telling friends and family members that they were going to the Yukon in search of work. Over the next seven days, they murdered a young couple whose van had broken down and, four days later, a 64-year-old man. On August 7, police found the bodies of both boys, who had committed suicide on or around that day. They also found videos the two left behind, taking full responsibility for the murders in an apparent bid for notoriety.

Are they serial killers? Technically, yes. The pair killed multiple people (at least two) over a four-day period (different times), and in different places. Their victims were strangers, and the murders appear to be premeditated. These are all common characteristics of male serial killers.

But their psychological profiles—obsession with military-battle video games, and collecting of Nazi paraphernalia, and Schmegelsky's father's description of his son as an angry, emotionally-scarred young man who, he suspected, wanted to go out in "a blaze of glory"—seems more consistent with a school shooter. Their lives did not return to normal between murders but appeared to be consumed by a continuous rampage that ended in suicide (very atypical for serial murderers). It's almost as if they were on-the-move mass murderers. These two would likely be classified as spree killers if the term was still in use.

7. How Do Police Know When a Serial Killer Is On The Loose? The easiest way a serial killer is identified is through DNA, fingerprints, or some other physical evidence the perpetrator leaves at two or more crime scenes; when these match, cops know the same person was involved or responsible. Interestingly, though, physical evidence is left behind at only 50 percent of serial crime scenes. So, police have to look for other clues.

One possible clue is similar crime-scene behaviors, such as the level of planning involved, location of the crime, level of violence, and the degree to which the murder itself was act-focused (a means to an end, such as the elimination of a witness after a rape) or process-focused (such as the use of torture or strangling to satisfy a sexual need). Many serial killers engage in rituals with their victims, behaviors that aren't necessary to kill but are done to satisfy some psychological need. So, for instance, the serial killer might take a piece of clothing or jewelry from each victim, might pose the body in some way, or only kill lovers parked in cars.

For investigators to be able to link crimes together, the crime-scene behaviors must be unique enough to separate them from other killers and consistent enough across crimes that investigators recognize that this is the same perpetrator. A serial killer who routinely took his victims' jewelry would be significant—since most murderers do not—but not unique in that sexual serial killers often take "trophies" from their victims. A serial killer who always left a red bandana tied to his victim's left foot might be.

Some serial killers' rituals are so unique that they become a signature—almost like a calling card. John Wayne Gacy would stuff the victim's underwear in his mouth. Suspected serial killer Deangelo Martin, awaiting trial for four counts of first-degree murder in 2018 and 2019, likes to leave behind one of his victims' socks at the scene of the crime, while, in Greece, another killer stabbed each of four elderly prostitutes exactly four times in the neck. Charles Albright removed the eyes of each of the three prostitutes he killed in 1990 and 1991.

Of course, signatures can be forged. One of the most unique signatures was that of the Zodiac, a serial killer who, over a five-year period (1969-74) in the San Francisco area, used a knife and gun to take the lives of at least seven strangers. Most of his victims were young couples. His signature was sending local newspapers and police departments taunting letters with parts of a cipher that he said, if decoded, would contain his identity; he also closed each letter with a symbol consisting of a cross with a circle in it. The Zodiac Killer was never identified.

As such, when, in the early 1990s in New York City, three random people were murdered on the streets with a note close to their bodies describing each victim's astrological sign, predicting future zodiac-related murders, and claiming to be the San Francisco Zodiac, investigators feared the San Francisco killer had moved to the Big Apple.

A handwriting comparison across posts quickly debunked this theory and, in 1996, Eddie Seda was charged with three murders and one attempted murder. Ironically, the same handwriting that eliminated him as the California Zodiac ended his career as a New York copycat. Seda had originally been arrested after shooting his half-sister and it was the similarities between his confession to this crime, and the letters he had sent police following his stranger-murders, that pointed to his candidacy as a potential serial killer.

Unfortunately, from a catch-the-bad-guy perspective, most serial killers don't have signatures. And their rituals can change over time. However, we're finding that, even if the specific rituals changes, the underlying need—for domination, for control, for humiliation—tends to remain the same. So investigative analysts look for common themes among similar crimes to see if more than one perpetrator might be involved.

Does England Have a Newly Discovered Serial Killer?

Time will tell. In 2020, a coroner in Cheshire, England was so disturbed by the crime scenes of five alleged murder-suicides of elderly couples between 1999 and 2011 that she drafted a 176-page independent report suggesting there may be a serial killer at work. Apparently, the coroner's predecessor had shared these concerns before her retirement.

Sadly, murder-suicides among the elderly are not uncommon so it was not unexpected that the initial conclusion was murder-suicide. In addition, many of the couples had risk factors (serious physical illness, caregiver stress) and had seemed depressed and overwhelmed to relatives.

However, two things raised the coroners' alarm. One, their relationship did not fit the typical relationship profile. Contrary to popular belief, most murder-suicides are not the result of a suicide pact or an act of mercy; they typically involve a depressed, controlling husband and an ill wife with a pending separation or change in living arrangement that triggers the violence. There is a pre-existing history of domestic violence in thirty to forty percent of these cases.

Two was the level of violence at the scene of the crime. Most elderly murder-suicide perpetrators shoot or (less common but not rare) stab their spouse and turn the murder weapon on themselves. In these cases, however, the wife was brutally butchered, often in several different ways—stabbed with a knife and hit in the head with a hammer and suffocated with a pillow. Husbands were found strangled, suffocated and stabbed beside them. On at least two occasions, the wife's nightgown had been pushed up to her waist, suggesting the possibility of a sexual element to the crime scene.

Another reason to look beyond murder-suicide in these cases was not only the lack of premorbid violence or aggression between the husband and wife, but the absolute devotion surviving family members described between the married couple. The reaction to the report has been mixed; some family members insist it was extreme situational stress that led to a genuine murder-suicide, while some insist that not only would the husband never kill his beloved wife in such a brutal fashion, but his own physical frailty would have made him incapable of it. To date, police have been reluctant to investigate and the original verdicts stand.

8. Who Was the First Serial Killer? To answer this question, we have to go back hundreds of years and start with poison, clearly the most popular murder weapon in the old days. And I'm talking way back; one of the earliest examples of serial murders dates to 331 BC. In fact, there were so many poisoners milling about during Roman times that murder seemed to be run-of-the-mill.

According to Roman historian, Titus Livius Patavinus ("Livy"), a group of one hundred and seventy women used the plague as an alibi for poisoning lots of Roman men. The story goes that many prominent Roman men were dying in a surprisingly similar fashion. Roman citizens initially chalked up this unfortunate sequence of events to an epidemic that had been plaguing Rome that year until a servant girl approached the Senate and spilled the beans. An investigative team followed her to a house where twenty noblewomen were busy making potions that they then insisted were healthy concoctions. When challenged to prove it, they drank the potions and immediately died. However, it should be noted that Livy wrote this story down three hundred years after it happened, and his version is subject to interpretation. So, perhaps this tale should be taken with a grain of salt.

The first recorded solo female serial killer was also a poisoner, a woman named Locusta of Galt, who worked for the Roman emperor Nero's mother, Agrippina the Younger. She was tasked with poisoning members of the Imperial Family as well as Agrippina's husband, the former Emperor Claudius, as a means for Nero to gain power. It should be noted that, common or not, poisoning was a risky business as sooner or later many of them either poisoned the wrong person (a vengeful relative sought justice) or the person they poisoned for decided to tie up some loose ends; Agrippina was eventually murdered by her ungrateful son, Emperor Nero.

A good candidate for the first male serial killer lived in China in the second century B.C.: Prince Liu Pengli, a member of the Han Dynasty's imperial family and king of the city of Jidong and its surrounding district starting in

144 B.C. Pengli was a sadistic brute who enjoyed hunting humans for fun. During his twenty-three-year reign of terror, he robbed and murdered at least one hundred people, leaving his subjects so terrified that they were afraid to come out of their homes at night.

Fast-forward a few thousand years and across oceans, and the first recorded U.S. serial killer was Dr. Henry Howard ("H. H.") Holmes. Born Herman Webster Mudgett on May 16, 1861 to a well-to-do and loving family, he unfortunately demonstrated a criminal mindset at an early age and, in addition to murder, was a bigamist, pathological liar, fraudster, and scammer. His killing spree was from 1891 to 1894; while he confessed to twenty-seven murders, he was convicted of nine.

9. How Many People Are Killed by a Serial Killer Each Year? Let's do some math. In 2018 (the most recent data we have), there were five homicides for every 100,000 people. The U.S. population that year was 327 million. If we divide 327,000,000 by 100,000 and then multiple it by five, we get 16,350 murders. The FBI estimates that the percentage of homicides committed by serial killers today is less than one percent. One percent of 16,350 would be 163 people. So, a good estimate would be that around 150 people are killed by a serial murderer each year. Practically speaking, you have a lot more to fear from the person sharing your bed than a person hiding underneath it. In contrast to the minuscule number of serial killer murder victims each year, 12.5 percent of murders are committed by victims' family members.

10. What Is the Most Common Weapon Used by Serial Killers? It's a common assumption that serial killers like to murder in an up-close-and personal fashion. However, from a popularity standpoint, serial killers in the United States rely on their guns. Shootings account for nearly half of the estimated 10,000 murders attributed to twentieth-century serial kills. The first runner-up is strangulation at 22 percent and stabbing is third at around 15 percent. However, the choice of a weapon often depends on the motive of the murderer and the gender of the victim; sexually motivated serial killers prefer to strangle their female victims and bludgeon or stab the males.

A Car as a Serial Killer's Murder Weapon?

It's not unusual for serial murderers—especially sexual serial killers—to use their cars as "accomplices" to lure their victims (for example, by offering a ride), imprison their victims (altering the locks or removing the door handles to make it escape-proof) or even kill them inside their vehicles. However, it is *not* common for a serial killer to use his automobile as the actual murder weapon. Recently arrested 32-year-old Lawrence Paul Mills III appears to be an exception.

Here's how Mills operated. First, he would choose a sex worker from Detroit's seedy south side. After approaching her, he would pay for sex and they would have it inside his car. However, after the deed was done and she got out of the car, Mills would trail his victim in his car and run over her. He would then calmly get out and take back the money he'd paid for sex. All of his attacks, resulting in the deaths of two women and an unborn child as well as another attempted murder, took place between October and December 2017.

11. How Many Active Serial Killers Are There in the U.S.? Obviously, we have no way to know because, well, they haven't been caught yet. That doesn't prevent us from guessing, though! Using case linkages made by journalists and law enforcement and requiring three murders instead of two (the older victim-count requirement), criminologist Kenna Quinet estimates there are about one hundred and fifteen serial killers dating back to the 1970s in the United States who have (so far) escaped justice. (In comparison, there were six hundred and twenty-five solved serial-murder cases in the same time frame). Of course, Quinet has no idea how many of these are still alive.

The FBI currently estimates that the number of serial killers has decreased by 85 percent over the past thirty years in the U.S. and is currently down to somewhere between 25 and 50 active serial murderers. (In comparison, there were one hundred and fifty-one in 1994.) However, not everyone agrees.

Some experts think what has changed is the number of serial killers *who have gotten caught.* In 1965, the U.S. homicide rate was virtually identical to what it was in 2018 (5.1 per 100,000 versus 5 per 100,000) but the 1965 U.S. homicide clearance rate was 91 percent. In 2017, it was 61.6 percent, one of the lowest rates in the Western world. In other words, in two out of every five homicides, the perpetrator gets away with murder.

Thomas Hargrove, the founder of the Murder Accountability Project, a nonprofit that collects data on homicide and looks for serial patterns, has analyzed how many unsolved murders are linked by DNA evidence. He believes that at least two percent of murders are committed by serial offenders—translating to about 2,100 unidentified serial killers. He has some data to support him; he arrived at this estimate after looking at how many unsolved murders had been linked to another murder through DNA. The answer was 1,400, or a little more than two percent of their files.

There's obviously a huge difference between 50 and 2,100. My guess is that the truth is somewhere in between.

12. What Serial Killer Has Had the Most Victims? Samuel Little currently holds the U.S. title and it is unlikely he will lose it any time soon. His killing spree spanned thirty-five years (1970-2005), covered fourteen states, and claimed as many as ninety-three victims (sixty of which have been confirmed). Although he was arrested over one hundred times for a variety of offenses and was actually tried and acquitted of one murder, he spent less than ten years in prison before he was linked by DNA to three murders in LA in 2012.

There is debate as to holds the "world record." Columbian serial killer Pedro Lopez was sentenced for raping and killing one hundred and ten young girls, although it is believed he killed up to three hundred between 1969 and 1980. Most of his victims were nine to twelve years old.

Another candidate is Luis Garavito, who, in 1999, admitted to the rape, torture and murder of one hundred and thirty-eight boys and teenagers; this body count is also believed to be an underestimate. In the U.K., a mild-mannered and popular physician and healthcare serial killer, Harold Shipman, M.D., murdered at least two hundred and fifteen of his patients and is suspected of knocking off up to two hundred and fifty. As far as female serial killers over the past hundred and fifty years, the title would go to our previously mentioned baby killer Amelia Dyer.

Guinness World Record Holder for Most Prolific Female Serial Killer—or Not?

Let's travel back in time, back to the end of the 1500s/early 1600s. Meet Hungarian Countess Elizabeth Bathory, an evil, vain woman who bathed in the blood of her young victims in an effort to retain her vitality and beauty. In 1610, she was found guilty of torturing and murdering eighty young girls and thought to have killed over six hundred. Even today, she holds the world record as the most prolific female serial murderer.

No one cared what the Countess was doing as long as she confined her escapades to servants; it was only when she ran out of poor people to torture and murder and set her sights on nobles' daughters that she was arrested. Even then, her only punishment was to be locked in a room in her castle with small slits for food and air; not a pleasant fate, but certainly a mild one given the pain she caused others. There she lived for three years, dying in August 1614.

It sure makes for a good story. The problem is that, from the very beginning, accounts were influenced by politics and intrigue. Some of her accusers owed her money which they did not want to pay. Many of the witnesses against her had no evidence and simply recounted things they had heard or been told by others. Several of Bathory's own servants were tortured and we all know how torture can loosen lips (although not necessarily with the truth). The six hundred-plus murders to which she is credited were reported by one woman who claimed to have seen a diary kept by the Countess listing all of her victims. (This diary was never found and, given the absolute indifference with which nobility viewed serfs, it is highly unlikely that she would recognize many of them by name. And the infamous story about her bathing in blood did not appear until over one hundred years after her death.

So, the likelihood of all this being true is practically zero. However, it *is* likely that Countess Bathory was a mean and abusive master; in 1602, a priest wrote a documented letter outlining a number of cruelties committed by the Countess and her husband, Count Nadasdy (who died before Bathory was brought to justice). Given the general leeway nobles were given to mistreat their serfs at this time, a letter documenting mistreatment suggests she was way more than your average tyrant.

13. What Country Has Had the Most Serial Killers?

The answer to this question will probably surprise no one. Between 1900 and 2016, there have been 3,204 serial killers in the good old U.S.A., followed distantly by England at 166. That means for every serial killer in the U.K., there have been twenty here at home. Contrary to popular belief, however, Americans aren't especially bloodthirsty in general; when you compare the overall murder rate in the U.S. with other countries, we're right around the middle.

Any way you look at it, that doesn't speak particularly well of some of our ancestors. But why would American citizens be so over-represented among the world's serial murderers? I've often wondered if our cultural values around individualism (valuing independence, self-reliance, and standing out/being unique)—which have many benefits and strengths—get perversely applied by disturbed Americans with murder on their mind. Sure, there are serial killers in every country, but perhaps U.S. murderers are more motivated to be the "best."

But here's something to consider: It may not simply be that the U.S. has a knack for breeding serial killers, it may be that, in comparison to other countries, we are exceptionally good at finding them. It's not always easy to link crimes to the same perpetrator, which is the first step in stopping a serial killer. To do that, you need competent law-enforcement agencies, which the U.S. has.

Then, once the serial killer has been captured, he has to be convicted and the conviction made public. In the U.S., we tend to be much more transparent than many other countries in acknowledging our criminal citizens. In contrast, leaders in the former Soviet Union proclaimed their "Socialist paradise" as completely free of "decadent Western crimes" like serial murder and, as such, turned a blind eye while running amok were serial killers like Vasili Ivanovich Komarov (the "Wolf of Moscow" who was convicted of killing twenty-nine people in Moscow between 1921 and 1923), Vladimir Ionesyan ("the MosGaz Killer", a Soviet actor who murdered three boys and two women with an ax in 1963 and 1964), and Boris Gusakov (the "Student Hunter," who committed six murders and fifteen violent sexual assaults on young women and girls between 1964 and 1968).

14. What State Has Produced the Most Serial Killers?
Just to count serial killers by state seems unfair since states with a much lower population would have an edge in terms of avoiding this illustrious dishonor. To compensate for this, the FBI tallies its count by looking at the number of serial killings in comparison to the number of residents. If you calculate it that way, Alaska comes out on top, with 15.65 serial killings per one million inhabitants. Fifty-one serial

murders took place in Alaska between 1900 and 2014, with more than half of those occurring between 1980 and 1990.

If your goal is to avoid states with the most serial-killer victims (regardless of population), steer clear of California, Florida, and Texas and head toward South Dakota, Hawaii, or New Hampshire. California, in particular would be a place to cross off your vacation list. Between 1980 and 1990, California serial killers were responsible for one-fifth of the 2,670 murders nationwide. California still tops the list; since 1900, 1,628 of its residents have been murdered by a serial killer.

The Traveling Man (and Serial Killer)

What state gets "credit" if a serial murderer commits murders in Florida, Georgia, *and* New York? That's a tough question to answer; most likely the state in which the serial killer lives. Twenty years ago, that question wouldn't have even been asked because the prevailing thought was that serial killers stuck close to home.

While most serial killers do murder in a limited geographical area in which they are familiar and feel comfortable, back in 2004 an Oklahoma Bureau of Investigation analyst noticed a pattern of murdered women being found along a major highway (I-40) that cut across multiple states.

When the FBI took a closer look, they found a similar patten along other major highways and began looking at suspects whose job would take them along major interstate routes—long-haul truck drivers. Not only did they discover a number of transient serial killers who murdered across state lines, they've uncovered four hundred and fifty potential murder suspects (many of them long-haul truck drivers) and seven hundred and fifty murder victims since their Highway Serial Killings Initiative began.

According to researcher Ginger Strand in her book *Killer on the Road*, at least twenty-five truck drivers are currently behind bars for serial murder. Samuel Legg III is one of the most recent long-haul truck drivers to be suspected of serial murder. Currently in an Ohio forensic psychiatric hospital after being found not competent to stand trial, he is suspected in the unsolved rape of a 17-year old girl and murders of four women between 1992 and 1997, including his 14-year-old stepdaughter. He was arrested in 2019 after DNA evidence connected him to the crimes.

Of course, most truck drivers aren't serial killers and you don't have to be a truck driver to murder in multiple states. A number of serial killers have moved around, collecting victims along the way: Ted Bundy (Washington, Utah, Colorado, and Florida), team serial killers Kenneth Bianchi and his cousin Angelo Buono Jr. (Los Angeles, Washington), and Samuel Little (multiple states, including California, Texas, Florida, Georgia, Ohio, Mississippi, Illinois, Tennessee, Louisiana, Arkansas, Kentucky, Maryland and Arizona).

15. What U.S. City or Region Holds the Record for the Most Serial Killers? As far as I know, no U.S. agency tracks serial killers by city. From a common-sense perspective, it would seem that serial killers would be most attracted to large cities, where they can blend in anonymously and have a diverse and large victim pool to choose from. New York

City has certainly had its fair share of serial murderers: David Berkowitz (1976-77), Eddie Seda (1990-93), Joel Rifkin (1989-93), Robert Shulman (1991-95), and the still-elusive Gilgo Beach killer (1996-?). In the 1980s, Los Angeles had at least five serial killers acting *at* the same time.

No one, though, can explain why a small college town was such a serial killer magnet in the 1970s. In February 1973, after four young men were discovered in a makeshift cabin in California's Henry Cowell Redwoods State Park, the district attorney of Santa Cruz County described his jurisdiction as "the murder capital of the world." Those four murders in the second month of 1973 brought the total homicides in Santa Cruz County up to thirteen for the year. The city of Santa Cruz in the 1970s had a population of between 30,000 to 40,000 but it certainly was a hotbed of serial-killing, with John Linley Frazier (the Killer Prophet), Edmund Kemper (the Co-ed Killer), and Herbert Mullin all targeting victims in and around the city.

The Serial Capital of Canada

Just as it's strange to think of Santa Cruz, California as a hotbed of serial killers, so, too, is it to consider London, Ontario, a beautiful university town of 383,822 by last count (averaging, however, just 170,000 residents at the time of the murders) located two hours southwest of Toronto as a candidate for the Serial Killer Capital of Canada.

According to a leading serial killer researcher, Michael Arntfield, as many as six serial killers were operating in the Canadian town between 1960 and 1985, committing up to twenty-nine murders. Thirteen of the solved ones were committed by three serial killers: Gerald Thomas Archer (1969-71, responsible for the murder of three female hotel employees); Russell Maurice Johnson (1973-77, found to be insane and committed to a forensic psychiatric hospital for killing three women although he confessed to seven murders and eleven sexual assaults); and Christian Magee (1974-76, a sexually sadistic murderer convicted of killing three women).

While no arrests have been made in the remaining cases, Arntfield believes he has identified two other serial killers responsible for some of these cold cases and thinks there may be two more who have never been identified. If he's right, this would mean London, Ontario had one serial killer for every 28,333 citizens. This would be the per-capita equivalent of Los Angeles having one hundred and thirty-seven active serial killers operating simultaneously.

16. Who Was the Youngest Serial Killer? In June 2007, eight-year-old Amardeep Sada (also known as Amarjeet) took the lives of three babies in his small village in Bihar, India, including his one-year-old baby sister and six-month-old cousin. He had committed his first murder a year earlier, at age seven, but his family had kept it quiet. It wasn't until he took the six-month-old daughter of one of the villagers out to a field and beat her to death with a brick that authorities were called in. He apparently targeted babies because they were small and defenseless.

After his arrest, Sada was assessed by several psychologists. One found that he was a developing sadist who showed no remorse and whose violence would likely escalate. Another disagreed, arguing that there was no evidence of prolonged torture or other indicators of sadism. By the end of the evaluation, the consensus was that Sada had conduct disorder, a behavioral and emotional disorder that emerges in childhood or adolescence and is characterized by severe antisocial and aggressive behavior, including physical aggression, theft, property damage, and violation of others' rights. If left untreated, it can lead to antisocial personality disorder, with or without psychopathic features.

The next question was what to do with him. Sada was too young to be convicted of a crime (by Indian law) but no one thought he should simply be returned to his home. He was ultimately sent to a psychiatric facility for three years and then a children's home until age eighteen. He was released in 2016 and that's the last anyone has heard of him—so far. He may be living in India under an assumed name.

What Do We Do With Serial Killers Old Enough to Kill but Too Young to Die?

Violent U.S. teens pose a special challenge. With our traditional law-and-order mentality, the historical response has been to lock the door and throw away the key. In fact, before 2005, a juvenile could be sentenced to death and up until 2012, they could be sentenced to life without parole. This shift from send-them-away to second chances was primarily due to the increased courtroom acceptance of brain science, which has clearly demonstrated that a teenager's brain is different from adults. We now know that the structure of the brain continues to evolve until around age twenty-five and, in comparison to adults, decision-making and problem-solving among teenagers is influenced more by the brain's emotion centers (the amygdala) than centers that control logic (the prefrontal cortex).

This increased reliance on science to guide legal decisions seemed like a step forward and, generally speaking, it is. The problem is that there is a small subset of juveniles who are so repeatedly and viciously violent that to unleash them on society at age twenty-one (when many criminals are reaching their stride) is terrifying.

Back in the day, Jesse Pomeroy was one of those teens. In 1876, the 14-year-old was convicted of two counts of first-degree murder for the deaths of 10-year-old Katie Curran and four-year old Horace Millen. Initially sentenced to death, his sentence was commuted to life in solitary confinement. He spent forty-one years in prison before he died.

That would never happen today. In 1987, Rhode Island native, Craig Price, was thirteen years old when he committed his first murder; he was fifteen when he killed two more. Because of the laws at the time, he could only be held until age twenty-one. Fortunately, due to his horrendous behavior behind bars—including the attempted murder of another inmate—he was sentenced to an additional twenty-five years behind bars in 2019.

17. Who Was the Oldest Serial Killer (in Terms of When They Started Killing)? Serial killing tends to be a young man's business. While there have been occasional serial killers who have continued to kill past retirement age (Samuel Little, for example, committed his last murder at age sixty-five), it is extremely rare for someone to *start* their murderous career as a senior citizen.

Ray and Faye Copeland are exceptions. They developed their appetite for murder in their twilight years. While no one knows the exact date of their first murder, it is believed that

Ray was at least sixty-five. (Faye was seven years younger than her husband). Not that the Copelands were model citizens beforehand; Ray had been making a living selling stolen livestock since he was twenty years old. In fact, it seems as if the Copelands moved on to murder after running out of new livestock-selling schemes; over the years, he had progressed from personally stealing and selling stolen livestock to using drifters to buy livestock with bad checks. The problem was these drifters kept getting arrested and the trail would lead back to the Copelands.

After a two-year stint in the slammer for writing bad checks in the late 1970s, Ray apparently decided the farmhand drifters he was using in his scams were a loose end that needed to be eliminated to avoid further prison opportunities, so he began killing his co-conspirators after they had served their purpose at the cattle auctions. However, in 1989, a former farmhand told police he had seen human bones and a skull at the Copeland farm and the jig was up.

Police found a mountain of incriminating evidence when they investigated—the human remains of five farmhands, the 22-caliber Marlin bolt-action rifle that was used to shoot each victim in the back of the head, and a homemade quilt from the clothing of the deceased men. It was this latter item, along with a farm ledger in Faye Copeland's handwriting with an X next to twelve men's names, that doomed Faye in the courtroom. And so, in 1990 and 1991 respectively, the oldest serial-killing couple became the oldest death-row inmates.

18. Has a Serial Killer Ever Killed in More Than One Country? Yes, and his name was Jack

Unterweger. In 1974, the Austrian native strangled to death an 18-year-old German woman, Margaret Schäfer, with her own bra. Two years later, he was convicted and sentenced to life in prison. This might have been a just end to a horrible story except for Jack's literary talent; his prison writings caught the attention of writers, journalists and artists, who believed his writings (including an autobiography, *Purgatory or The Trip to Prison: Report of a Guilty Man*) signaled not only a rare talent but a reformed man.

In 1985, his literary champions began a campaign to get him pardoned and released. Because of a court-mandated 15-year minimum sentence, Unterweger remained behind bars until May 1990, at which time he was embraced with open arms. He became a celebrity; his book was taught in schools, and his children's stories were performed on Austrian radio. In essence, he became the poster child for prison rehabilitation, hosting television programs on the subject and covering crime stories for the public broadcaster ORF.

You probably see where this is headed. In 1991, Unterweger was hired by an Austrian magazine to travel to L. A. and write about crime and the differences between U.S. and European attitudes to prostitution. He met with local police, even going so far as to participate in a ride-along of the city's red-light districts. Shortly thereafter, three sex workers were beaten, sexually assaulted, and strangled to death with their own bras.

Law enforcement later found that Unterweger had killed a sex worker in Czechoslovakia, and seven more in Austria in 1990 in the first year after his release. All were garroted with their bras. On June 29, 1994, he was sentenced to life in prison without possibility of parole. That night, Unterweger committed suicide by hanging himself with a rope made from shoelaces and a cord from the trousers of a track suit, using the same knot that was found on all the strangled prostitutes.

There is more than one cautionary tale in this story, not the least of which is never mistake talent for virtue or writing skills for evidence of rehabilitation.

Part 2: Inside the Serial Killer's Psyche.

It typically takes a perfect storm of biology, traumatic childhood events, and adverse life experiences to create a serial killer. We're still trying to figure out what kind of storms lead to what kinds of violence.

19. What Causes Someone to Become a Serial Killer?

Ah, the million-dollar question. If we had the answer, they would be extinct because we could identify budding serial killers and stop them in their tracks. Unfortunately, there is no single recipe for a serial killer. But, while the road each serial killer travels to his first murder is unique, there are some commonly shared stops along the way; childhood trauma (60-75 percent), head injuries (about 20 percent), dysfunctional families, and social isolation.

These commonalities are nothing new; we've known about them for years. What *is* new is that we are beginning to identify what specific types of abuse (physical, psychological or sexual) are likely to lead down the road to what motives (money, lust, anger, etc.) and what specific types of violence (for example, torture, binding, overkill). If we can link specific early-childhood traumas to specific motives and crime-scene behaviors, this could help us narrow down a list of suspects. Although we are in the early stages of this work, a 2020 study found a link between serial killers who were sexually abused as children and the use of binding, torture, and mutilation of their later victims, while serial killers with a history of physical abuse were more likely to engage in "overkill" (for example, stabbing a victim one hundred times when one thrust of the knife would do the job).

Of course, there are thousands of people who suffered one—or all—of these life experiences and turned out just fine. It's not just what happens to you in childhood that shapes who you are; it's who you were before your childhood began, what you think about what happened to you, how you cope with what happens to you and what happens to you the rest of your life. As former FBI behavioral analyst and current criminal profiler, Jim Clemente, is fond of saying, "Genetics load the gun, personality and psychology aim it, and your experiences pull the trigger." And no matter what misfortunes they suffer growing up, at some point serial killers make choices and it is those choices for which they are responsible.

20. What Biological Factors May Predispose a Serial Killer to Violence? When you look at the ongoing debate about nature versus nurture in explaining why we humans behave as we do, the pendulum seems to swing back and forth. It's not that we psychologists don't recognize that both play a role (and, in fact, there's some fascinating research that suggests that certain environments can actually influence the development of the brain and vice versa); we do. It's the emphasis that's given to one or the other that shifts. One decade, the prevailing theory tends to focus on biology, genetics, temperament; the next, it's what happens to us after we exit the birth canal.

When it comes to explaining violence, the pendulum currently appears to be in nature's court. For instance, Dr. Helen Morrison has studied one hundred and thirty serial killers and believes that a chromosomal abnormality, such as an extra X or Y chromosome in their DNA, might act as a possible trigger for murderous behavior. One of her examples is serial killer Bobby Joe Long. Long, who was executed by lethal injection in Florida on May 23, 2019, sexually assaulted and murdered at least ten women in the Tampa Bay area between March and November 1984. He had an extra X chromosome in his DNA, resulting in an increase in his estrogen level.

Through his brain imaging of violent offenders, neuroscientist Jim Fallon has found that a low level of activity in the brain's orbital cortex is often found in psychopaths. His theory is that a deficit in this area of the brain, which is associated with ethical behavior, moral decision-making, and impulse control, makes it harder for psychopaths to suppress impulses of rage, violence, hunger, or sexual desire.

Interestingly, during his research, Fallon discovered that he himself had the perfect psychopathic brain after his own brain scan accidentally got mixed up with the killers he studied. (He also later discovered that he has quite a few murderers in his family tree.) He concluded that his loving family and nurturing environment inhibited the expression of his genetic predisposition toward psychopathy, lending some support to us optimists who argue that anatomy is not destiny.

Fallon also rediscovered the MAO-A gene, aka the "warrior gene," which has been linked with an increased risk of violence and aggression. When present, this gene allegedly causes a domino effect; it causes certain changes in the X-chromosome gene that produces the Monoamine Oxidase A enzyme, which affects the neurotransmitters serotonin, dopamine, and norepinephrine. These neurotransmitters play a key role in how we process and regulate our emotions. Fallon theorizes that it's the individuals with low levels of MAO enzyme that we have to worry about, especially those who are then exposed to an abusive or traumatizing childhood.

The Warrior (Gene) on Drugs

While there does appear to be a link between the low level of MAOA found in "warrior gene" carriers and violence, it gets a little tricky. This gene variation is pretty common; at least one study suggests that 40 percent of the population possesses it. So, there are probably thousands of us law-abiding citizens walking around with low MAOA and not even knowing it.

And of course, our environment still matters. Recent research has also suggested a link between "warrior gene" carriers and a particularly nasty (i.e., aggressive) response to intoxication with alcohol and amphetamines. Of course, we all know that being drunk and high rarely brings out the best in any of us. It might be worth it to err on the safe side....

21. How Do We Explain Serial Killers From a Stable Family Background? If you are like I was before I had kids, you might think that parents are pretty much responsible for everything—good or bad—their child ever does. If only it was that simple.

There is no question that families have a tremendous influence on the development of their child's psyche. I know adults who have struggled much of their lives to get over the trauma of an abusive childhood. I also know adults who, graced with loving, stable role models, seem to naturally possess empathy, resilience, and wisdom that many of us have spent a lifetime trying to acquire. On the other hand, we know adults who seem to rise above a horrible childhood like the mythical phoenix rises from the ashes—and we know adults who seem hellbent on trashing every advantage they were born with.

As we've seen, serial killers as a group are much more likely to come from a seriously abusive backdrop than law-abiding citizens are. But there are serial killers, like Richard Cottingham (aka "The Torso Killer," killed nine women between 1967 and 1989) and Randy Kraft (killed at least sixteen young men between 1971 and 1983), who seem to turn out bad in spite of loving parents, adoring siblings, and a bevy of childhood friends. In a few cases, there is evidence that a childhood head injury might have been a major contributor to a violence-prone personality; Cottingham was hit by a car when he was four years old and had a head injury that damaged his frontal lobes. In other cases, we don't have a clue.

Here's my best guess: A warm nurturing childhood can neutralize a certain amount of genetic preloading for violence. Individuals born with the genetic jackpot for peace and resilience can likely withstand a horrific upbringing without letting it warp their psyche. But there are likely environments so violence-filled and traumatic that they can pretty much squash those buds of empathy most of us are born with. And there may be a rare few, Cottingham and Kraft among them, whose genetic makeup is so flawed that it would take a miracle for them not to yield to a propensity for violence.

From Football Player to Serial Predator

Former Green Bay Packer training-camp player Randall Woodfield (the "I-5 killer") murdered at least seven people along Interstate 5, targeting victims from Northern California to Washington. During his five-month reign of terror (October 1980-February 1981), he robbed, raped and killed. He attacked women he knew as well as complete strangers, stabbing, beating, and shooting his victims.

Woodfield came from a good home. He grew up with his two older sisters in picturesque Otter Rock, Oregon on the Pacific Coast. His father was a manager with the phone company, and his mother was a housewife. He was a talented athlete, excelling at sports at Newport High School, where he played football, basketball, and ran track.

But his criminal proclivities seem to be as strong as his athletic talent. As a teenager, he got caught peeping into bedrooms and was once arrested for exposing himself to women. In college, he was arrested after ransacking the apartment of an ex-girlfriend and arrested numerous times—and twice convicted—for indecent exposure. After he was drafted and released by the Green Bay Packers in 1974, he started robbing women at knifepoint and forcing them to perform oral sex. His first murder victim was former high school classmate Cherie Ayers, with whom he had reconnected at his 10-year high school reunion; she was found raped, stabbed, and bludgeoned to death in her Portland apartment. He was ultimately linked via DNA to six murders along with an assortment of other crimes including rape, sodomy, attempted kidnapping, armed robbery, and illegal possession of firearms. But authorities believe he may have killed up to forty-four.

22. Are There Common Characteristics to Serial Killers as Young Children? There are plenty of serial killers—male and female—who started out as delightful children. Girls, in particular, don't seem to cause many problems growing up. While there is a small subset of at-risk girls whose childhood behavior mimics acting-out boys, one longitudinal study found that, as children, future violent female offenders were more likely to be depressed and anxious than angry and rebellious. Instead of getting in fights with peers, they withdrew from them. Instead of getting expelled from school for disruptive behavior, they were more likely to develop stomachaches or other physical symptoms to avoid going. As girls, these female offenders tended to be the quiet girls who faded into the woodwork and hid out in their rooms. Until they reached puberty and all hell broke loose.

Joanna Dennehy: Sensitive Kid, Serial-Killer Adult

Kathleen Dennehy describes her daughter, Joanna (who murdered three men and stabbed two more in a ten-day killing spree in Peterborough, England in March 2013) as a sweet, sensitive child who made good grades and played hockey during her elementary-school years. Her younger sister, Maria, described her as a smart, strong-willed and protective big sister who always made time for her and loved to play dress up and dolls.

However, both family members say Joanna's personality and behavior changed when she hit adolescence. By age fifteen, she was running away from home, doing drugs, and skipping school; this apparently escalated after her parents tried to stop her relationship with John Treanor, who was five years older than she was. After running away from home eight times, police refused to go look for her and, at sixteen, she left home—and school—for good, married Treanor, and had two daughters.

After years of cheating, self-harm, abusing drugs, and escalating violence, Dennehy committed her murders at age thirty-one. During her trial, she was diagnosed with a number of personality disorders (psychopathy, borderline personality disorder, antisocial personality disorder) as well as sadomasochism, a paraphilia in which a person gets sexual pleasure from the infliction of pain or humiliation.

23. Then there are those budding serial killers—most often boys—who raise red flags from the start. When I was in graduate school, I was taught that three childhood behaviors in particular could predict future violence and even serial murders. These three behaviors, which became known as the McDonald triad because of the man (James McDonald) who developed the theory, were animal cruelty, bedwetting (past age seven), and fire-setting.

Recent research, however, indicates that this psychological crystal ball has failed to live up to its promise in predicting future serial killers. Most serial killers do not, in fact, abuse animals as children. However, I've met plenty of violent offenders, including murderers, who were horrified at the thought of animal cruelty and would beat up a friend or a neighbor before they'd prey on a pet.

To be sure, McDonald was on to something. Some troubled children start out by torturing animals and it snowballs from there and a lot more serial killers are childhood animal abusers than the average Joe (or Jane). While less than five percent of U.S. children have intentionally hurt an animal, children receiving mental-health treatment have animal cruelty rates from 10 to 25 percent. One in four teens diagnosed with conduct disorder has abused animals. When FBI agents interviewed thirty-six serial killers, they found that 68 percent had extended bedwetting, 56 percent had set fires as kids and 36 percent had been cruel to animals. Jeffrey Dahmer (murdered seventeen boys and young men between 1978 and 1991), David Berkowitz (murdered six people in New York City in 1976 and 1977), Albert DeSalvo (confessed to murdering thirteen Boston women between 1962 and 1964), and Ted Bundy are just a few of the famous serial killers who began their crimes against humans with cruelty toward animals.

It turns out that certain kinds of animal cruelty at certain ages *are* a clear warning sign and, in some cases, a bright red flag. Children over the age of six or seven understand that it's not okay to hurt an animal and that doing so will cause the animal pain. When they do it anyway, in many cases, it's an indicator that the child has experienced, or witnessed, some kind of physical abuse. Statistics show that 30 percent of children who have witnessed domestic violence subsequently act out a similar type of violence against their pets. In the first university study on the subject, researchers interviewed Romanian teenagers and found that 86.3 percent thought it was "normal" to see homeless animals being abused or killed; they'd witnessed adults do it dozens of times. They also found a chilling link between these children who *witnessed* animal cruelty and later engage in violence. Children who see others hurt animals are more likely to hurt them, too, and then transfer their aggression to humans.

What we've learned about the McDonald triad over the past twenty years suggests that 1) even the presence of one of these behaviors *(assuming physical conditions and heredity have been excluded as causes of enuresis*) may signal either a dysfunctional home environment and/or a child with poor coping skills; and 2) it is rare that all three behaviors are exhibited by the same person, even among serial killers.

From a practical standpoint, this suggests that a child who wets the bed after age ten *might* benefit from a mental-health checkup and a child with one of the other two behaviors *definitely* would. We also know that there are other behaviors that are equally—or more—telling when it comes to predicting later violence, such as children who don't exhibit age-appropriate empathy, who bully other children, who steal, who lie, who force other children into sexual activity.

You Didn't Need a Crystal Ball to See Where This Kid Was Headed

Keith Hunter Jesperson, aka, the "Happy Face Killer," killed eight women between 1990 and 1995 in Washington, California, Wyoming and Oregon. Given his behavior during childhood, it's hard to imagine his arrest coming as a surprise to anyone. In fact, minus the bedwetting (which, as a marker for future violence, leaves a lot to be desired), he could literally have been a childhood model for McDonald's theory.

He began torturing animals as a young child of five or six, especially cats. This "hobby" appeared to be noticed and approved of by his alcoholic father, who himself was known to put them in a sack and drown them in the river, although the young Jesperson did get a licking after he killed his dad's pet duck with a rock. As he got older, Keith experimented with even more sadistic and cruel ways to hurt cats and gophers and dogs.

By age eleven, he had attempted his first murder. According to Jesperson, he had a peer named Martin who would often accompany his parents when they visited the Jespersons. After Martin allegedly blamed his misdeeds on Jesperson several times (resulting in the eleven-year-old being punished by his father), Jesperson beat him into unconsciousness; he later said the only reason he didn't kill him was because his father pulled him off. A similar event happened with another kid at a swimming pool; this time, the life guard intervened.

And, of course, Jesperson had a strange fascination with fires, something he shared with his grandfather. He set at least a few fires on the side of the highway and, at fourteen, was experimenting with pipe bombs. While no one can predict a serial killer from his childhood, he would have been a good one to put your money on.

24. Does Puberty Trigger Something Murderous in Serial Killers? No, but it doesn't make things easier. As many of us know firsthand, puberty does not bring out the best in most of us. With all those hormones flying around and peer relationships to navigate, most adolescents go through some degree of rebellion against parents and authority figures as well as some normal experimentation with boundaries and rules.

One of the trickiest things about looking back at the childhood of serial killers is that, since we know the end of their story, it's easy to make the beginning fit. In other words, it's easy to do some Monday morning quarterbacking, looking back on a serial killer's childhood and zeroing in on early behaviors that scream "future serial killer" when there are thousands of others who perhaps exhibited the same quirks or problems but never had a single homicidal thought. Childhood friend, Sandi Holt, said serial killer Ted Bundy liked to scare people; well, so did my youngest son! Samuel Little's first crime was stealing a bicycle at age sixteen; nothing there to indicate he'd go on to murder ninety-six women.

But there are some adolescent clues that, at the very least, foreshadow future violence; animal cruelty, bullying peers, getting into frequent and violent fights, early criminal activity, expulsion from school, heavy substance abuse. It is also during adolescence that most sexual serial killers began committing "beginner" sexual crimes such as voyeurism and exhibitionism, that escalate into more serious sexual offenses. Many sexual serial killers kill in their minds long before they move from fantasy to reality and it is often during adolescence that these deviant sexual and/or violent fantasies grow. We forensic psychologists need to do a better job of asking teens and adults who are referred for violent and/or sexual crimes about the nature of their sexual fantasies, their sexual history, and deviant sexual interests.

What about the girls? It's common to see budding female serial killers beginning with financial crimes—theft, shoplifting, fraud—and then move on to profit-motivated murders. We also tend to see a pattern of compulsive lying and attention-seeking start to emerge. Violence in teen girls tends to be more relational than physical, i.e., controlling others through social exclusion, gossip, and manipulating others to get what she wants. For example, female serial killer Velma Barfield's criminal career began when she began stealing pocket change from her father after noticing how much poorer she was than her friends; she wound up murdering between five and seven victims between 1969 and 1978. She was the first woman to be executed by lethal injection.

Which Troubled Teens Are Budding Serial Killers?

Swedish researcher Selma Salihovoc spent four years following 1,068 Swedish boys and girls in the seventh through ninth grades to see how much their psychopathic traits would change over time. Most of the teens started out with low to moderate levels of psychopathy which decreased even further as they got older. In other words, relatively few teens had psychopathic traits to begin with and, among those who did, they appeared to be temporarily inflated by developmental immaturity and improved over time.

This was not true, though, for a small group of teenagers. These adolescents had psychopathic traits at the start of the study and they didn't lessen over time. These were also the adolescents with the highest levels of misconduct, criminal behavior, and most problematic relationships with their parents. Given the link between adult psychopathy and violence, shouldn't we also assess it in teenagers as well? Clearly, these are youths we need to worry about.

From a case-by-case perspective, perhaps that should depend on the crime more than the perpetrator's age. If not tried as an adult, a teenager who commits a premeditated murder in an up-close-and-personal way, particularly when there is a clear pre-existing history of psychopathic behavior and/or sexual assault should, at the very least, be closely monitored well past the age at which he can buy a beer.

25. How Does Someone Become a Serial Killer and His Siblings Turn Out Just Fine? This is an interesting question and it's often used to argue against nurture as an explanation for serial murder. After all, if three kids all grow up in the same household and only one turns to murder, how can the way they were raised be to blame? The other kids turned out all right.

It's true that most serial killers (about eighty-five percent) have law-abiding (or at least non-murderous) siblings. Dennis Rader was the oldest of four boys, John Wayne Gacy had two sisters, Jeffrey Dahmer had a younger brother. But no matter how close, no two siblings are alike; there are biological differences—in temperament, personality, and ability—that influences how a child interacts with and interprets his environment.

It's also true that two people can grow up in the same family and have very different experiences. Perhaps one child is ridiculed while another is the "golden child"; Diane Staudte was so enamored with her favorite child, Rachel, that she collaborated with her to bump off the other three. Maybe one child excels at school and is praised and popular, while another has a learning difference and is bullied or rejected. It's a different experience living with stepparents or extended family; Ted Bundy grew up with a different father than his half-siblings while Myra Hindley was sent to live with her grandmother while her younger sister stayed with their mom. Even birth order can have an impact; the majority of serial killers are first-born, about twice as often as only children. Of course, none of these factors in and of themselves tip the scale to serial murder. But exposure to adverse events that a child experiences adds weight.

A Savior and a Slayer in the Same Family

Few families have experienced the horror and the heroism as the Stayner family. On December 4, 1972, seven-year-old Steven Stayner was walking home from school in Merced, California when he was lured into a car and abducted by child sex predator Kenneth Parnell. Parnell then convinced Steven that his parents no longer wanted him and had essentially given him to Parnell.

For the next seven years, Steven lived with his captor in Mendocino, California, three hundred miles away from his family and under a different name; he was repeatedly sexually and emotionally abused. However, when Parnell abducted a five-year-old boy with the intent to make him his new sex slave, fourteen-year-old Steven decided he was not going to let what had happened to him happen to another child. He decided to escape.

On March 1, 1980, the teenager waited until Parnell left for work, and then he and the young boy escaped. After making it to a local police station, law enforcement was eventually able to locate both boys' parents. Both were joyfully reunited with their families. Steven eventually married and had two children before dying in a motorcycle accident at age twenty-four. Before he died, he worked with child abduction groups and often spoke to children about stranger danger and personal safety.

It is unclear what impact Steven's disappearance had on his brother, Cary, or his three sisters. Undoubtedly, it was traumatic; as the oldest (and four years older than Steven), Cary must have felt a sense of guilt and responsibility over not protecting his brother. He later stated that, after his brother disappeared, he felt neglected by his parents, who were consumed by what had happened and that, after Steven returned, he was jealous of all the attention and gifts his younger brother received.

In July 1999, Cary Stayner was arrested for murdering four women in Yosemite Park, California over the previous year. Steven, child victim of a sexual predator, had a brother who was a sexually-motivated serial killer. It is a tragic irony that while Steven Stayner was enduring his horrific abuse, his father, Delbert, was ordered into therapy for sexually abusing his daughters and his older brother, Cary, was molested by his uncle. After his arrest, Cary told FBI Special Agent Jeffrey Rinek that while his brother's ordeal had been traumatizing, he had had fantasies of hurting young women and girls since age six.

So why did Steven Stayner go from victim to victim's advocate while his brother moved from victim to predator? That's something we're still trying to figure out.

26. What Links Are There Between Adoption and Serial Killing? As an adoptive mom, this is a hard one for me; one, because I have the four greatest kids (some adopted, some not) in the world and two, because there are so many issues mixed up in untangling the relationship between adoption and serial murder.

Some of the most notorious serial killers *were* adopted. David Berkowitz (a.k.a. Son of Sam), Ted Bundy, Aileen Wuornos, Joel Rifkin, and the Boston Strangler are just a handful of the prominent serial murderers who also happen to be adoptees. Of the five hundred estimated serial killers in

U.S. history, 16 percent were adopted as children, while adoptees represent only two or three percent of the general population. Adoptees are fifteen times more likely to kill one or both of their adoptive parents than biological children.

But correlation does not mean causation. In fact, there are so many confusing factors that it's impossible to determine the exact nature of the relationship—if any—between the two. First of all, adoptions were historically closed, leaving a child without any information about her birth family, ethnicity, or family history. Not knowing where they came from was, in and of itself, traumatic for some children.

A second complication is the circumstances surrounding the relinquishment of a child. As a group, U.S. children who are put up for adoption are more likely to come from families that are less stable and more likely to have a history of substance abuse, mental illness, and behavioral problems. (In some other countries, placement for adoption is more likely to be strictly for financial reasons). As such, the issue is not whether or not a child is adopted but what the child genetically brings to the table, what his or her adoptive parents contribute (biologically and through parenting), and what happens to him or her after s/he is adopted. In other words, it's complicated.

27. What Are the Most Common Motives of Serial Killers? If you're looking for complicated motives, you've come to the wrong place. Most serial killers commit their murders because they enjoy it. They love the thrill of the hunt, the rush of power enjoyed by control-oriented killers, or the pleasure derived from sexual sadists, but the bottom line is that most serial killers kill because it makes them feel good.

Don't overlook the seduction of cold, hard cash, however. It comes in a close second to psychological pleasure, with a tad over 30 percent of serial killers listing money as a major motivator. Think of the black-widow killer who cashes in on life insurance policies after she's sent her dearly departed spouse to the pearly gates or the landlady killer who keeps cashing her murdered tenants' Social Security checks. Let's not forget that many serial killers have multiple motives for what they do. This is true not just for solo serial murderers but also for team players.

A Hunter of Humans

> Robert Hansen was a serial killer from Alaska who would kidnap vulnerable women (exotic dancers, sex workers), rape them in his home, fly them into the wilderness in his private plane, and hunt them down like animals with his Ruger Mini-14 rifle and a knife. Many of his victims were blindfolded and naked when he let them loose. Between 1971 and 1983, he killed at least seventeen young women.
>
> He would have continued but met his match in June 1983 when he kidnapped 17-year-old Cindy Paulson. Not only did she manage to escape from his car while partially handcuffed as he was fueling up the airplane, she had memorized virtually everything about him during her captivity—directions to his house, what the secret basement looked like, etc. Robert Hansen took lives, but Cindy Paulson's courage saved many others.

28. How Can a Serial Killer Come Across as a Normal Person? It's amazing what human beings can do when our backs are up against the wall or we want something bad enough. Here's a minor example: In 1998, my mother died suddenly and unexpectedly when I was thirty-eight years old. I was devastated; not only was I in shock, but I had just signed a publishing deal for my first book. Somehow, I tucked away my grief and sadness, and spent the next three months feeling nothing and writing constantly. After the book was finished, I fell apart.

Serial killers who successfully lead double lives rely on a coping strategy we all use—compartmentalization. The difference is that we don't have such drastic discrepancies between different parts of ourselves, nor do we have so much at stake if one part of our lives bleeds over to the next. I think one reason some serial killers are so successful at putting up, and keeping, rigid mental boundaries between their serial-killing activities and other areas of their lives is because they have spent years living in their heads before they start killing. From an early age, many serial killers use fantasy to cope with a host of unpleasantries—abuse, loneliness, a sense of powerlessness. They fix their problems in their minds because, in the real world, they either can't or they don't know how. Fantasy is a self-protective strategy many children use when they are trapped in difficult or unbearable situations. When infused with rage, bad things happen.

As puberty hits, there is a small minority of troubled, often-abused teens whose fantasies take a dark turn. These are often teens whose difficult childhood is compounded by social and/or sexual dysfunction. Without an external outlet for their frustrations and longings, they increasingly turn inward. They tell themselves stories in which they are in control, they are calling the shots, they are making others pay.

They search for outlets for their deviant fantasies—violent pornography, an acceptable group to scapegoat. They put people into different categories—their circle of friends and family, with whom they behave decently, and individuals with whom they have no relationship and victimize with no feelings at all. This is how a sexual sadist can treat a sex worker or someone he meets in a bar in a way he wouldn't dream of treating a neighbor, friend, or loved one.

They also tell themselves stories that justify or rationalize what they have done; listen to serial killers' confessions on YouTube and you'll hear how the drug-using sex worker Samuel Little murdered "really wanted to die anyway" or how serial-killer nurse Elizabeth Wettlaufer thought God was directing her murders even though it was clear she was selecting most of her victims by how annoying or difficult they were.

They also take advantage of another universal human process; our ability to dehumanize people who are different than we are. Politicians have used this strategy for years to whip normal people into a frenzy and give them psychological permission to commit violence against a certain group. (Nazis, for example, referred to Jews as rats and vermin, while Hutu extremists who organized the Rwandan genocide called the Tutsi people cockroaches and snakes. Serial killers do the same; sex workers become "sex machines," gays become "AIDS carriers," homeless people are "trash." After all, they rationalize to themselves, what's wrong with getting rid of "garbage" or eliminating a "disease?"

Do "Normal" People Fantasize About Murder?

Time and again, we read stories about troubled individuals who waved a red flag of warning again and again before they killed. Friends noticed, families worried, and coworkers avoided this person who seemed to be a ticking time bomb. In some cases, people tried to intervene: a *New York Times* review of one hundred rampage killings found that thirty-four concerned families or friends had desperately tried to get the person help before the murders but had been unable to convince professionals to step in.

So how could mental-health professionals miss—or minimize—clear markers that signaled impending mayhem? One reason is that homicidal thoughts are not uncommon: In 2000, Peter Crabb and associates surveyed three hundred undergraduate students and found that *60 percent* of the males and 32 percent of the women could describe a recent murderous fantasy, most often in response to a relationship breakup or an interpersonal dispute. Few of us would be shocked to learn that a friend or colleague had entertained a fleeting homicidal urge when angry or hurt.

Second, most people with homicidal fantasies never act on them. Homicidal thoughts can be triggered by a number of circumstances, events, and feelings—jealousy, betrayal, rejection, interpersonal conflict, paranoid delusions, command auditory hallucinations, etc. The challenge for us mental-health professionals is to sort through which homicidal thoughts are most likely to lead to homicide. We do have some clues as to which ones are more likely to turn deadly; when there is a history of threats or violence, a specific and detailed plan, increasing and frequent homicidal thoughts, access to guns or other weapons, substance abuse is involved, and/or the person gets pleasure from the homicidal fantasies.

Persistent homicidal thoughts should *always* be evaluated. They don't necessarily mean that a person is going to kill someone, but they do mean *something*. Why not let a professional figure it out?

29. What Mental Illnesses Are Most Commonly Associated with Serial Killers? Let's get one thing straight; most violence is not caused by mental illness. The vast majority of people who have a serious mental illness are not violent and the vast majority of violent people are not mentally ill. Individuals with a serious mental illness are much more likely to kill themselves than someone else. With the exception of the previously mentioned and extremely rare visionary serial killer whose murders are a response to command auditory hallucinations ("you must make a human sacrifice or thousands of people will die in this catastrophic earthquake"), delusions ("these people are trying to poison me and my family so I must defend us") or both, it's not mental illness that enables most serial killers to do what they do; it's their lack of empathy, lack of guilt or remorse, lack of fear, grandiosity, deep-seated rage, and desire for power and control.

In fact, over half of serial killers have never received a psychiatric diagnosis. Of those who have, most have been diagnosed with one or more personality disorders; substance abuse is also common. The most frequently diagnosed personality disorder is antisocial personality disorder. Between two to three percent of the general population have antisocial personality disorder; in contrast, slightly less than half of all prison inmates meet the diagnostic criteria for this disorder. If you look at the diagnostic criteria, you'll quickly realize that many of the "symptoms" are law-breaking behavior; repeated lying, frequent physical fights or assaults, failure to fulfill financial obligations. As such, it's no surprise that you find a lot of these people in prison. Other personality disorders (borderline, narcissistic, or paranoid) are rarer but not uncommonly diagnosed in criminals.

The Poster Child for Psychopathy

Serial killer Peter Woodcock is a testament to the intractability of psychopathy and, perhaps, our early overconfidence in our ability to treat it. To be fair, by the time Woodcock started his killing career—while still in his teens—he had been exhibiting disturbing behavior for years. Born in 1939, he was sixteen when he killed his first victim, 6-year-old Wayne Mallette. Three weeks later, he strangled nine-year-old Gary Morris, and in January 1957, he murdered four-year-old Carole Voyce. Found not guilty by reason of insanity, he spent the next thirty-four years in a variety of forensic psychiatric hospitals undergoing experimental treatments for psychopathy.

On his *first* unsupervised release, Woodcock convinced a paroled murderer and former hospital-mate, Bruce Hamill, that an alien brotherhood would solve all of his problems if Hamill helped him kill another hospital inmate, Dennis Kerr. Together, they lured Kerr to a secluded spot and butchered him. Hamill went to sleep waiting for the aliens to appear while Woodcock walked into town and turned himself in. After his death in 2010, Woodcock was described in the *Toronto Star* as "the serial killer they couldn't cure."

Unlike serial killers, though, most inmates do not meet the diagnostic criteria for antisocial personality disorder *with psychopathy*, a particularly nasty combination of manipulative and exploitive behavior alongside an inability to feel guilty, remorse or empathy. A number of serial killers have been diagnosed as psychopaths, including Ted Bundy, John Wayne Gacy, and

Charles Manson. (In 2007, a group of seventy-two psychologists did a postmortem analysis of Ted Bundy's personality and 95 percent also added narcissistic personality disorder to the mix).

Without a doubt, all serial killers act psychopathically towards their victims; they are manipulative, deceitful, do illegal and harmful things, and without empathy or remorse. Some seem incapable of forming attachments to anyone and truly seem to lack any capacity to feel remorse, guilt, compassion, or empathy for anyone. Any hint of humanity or genuine emotion seems to be part of a carefully constructed persona, the infamous "mask" in which true psychopaths hide their devious and deviant desires.

Others, however, appear to genuinely care about their family and friends but draw a red line between their regular life and their lethal "leisure activities" and between their victims and their family and friends. For these killers, it may not be that they hide behind a mask but that their psyches are so fragmented that each part seems completely separate from each other.

And then there's the issue of sex. Some serial killers have deviant sexual appetites that are atypical or extreme enough to be a diagnosable paraphilia. With a paraphilia, "normal" sexual arousal and gratification gets linked to unusual things or unusual behaviors and either causes the person distress (for example, by causing problems in his relationships) or puts others in harm's way (such as with pedophilia). Paraphilias don't always involve illegal activity; getting sexually aroused by shoes, for instance, doesn't mean someone is going to shoplift. Some people who get off on inflicting pain on others (sadism) find a consensual partner who gets off by experiencing it.

Other paraphilias, however, can't be expressed in a law-abiding way. Some paraphilias such as necrophilia (sexual attraction toward corpses), pedophilia (sexual attraction toward children) or frotteurism (sexual arousal through touching or rubbing up against a nonconsenting adult) are often referred to as "criminal paraphilias" because of their link to criminal behavior. And sexual sadism is much more common in sexual serial killers than among normal adults or other kinds of sex offenders.

Jerry Brudos and his Killer Shoe Fetish

Serial killer Jerome Henry Brudos, who murdered at least four Oregon women during 1968 and 1969, earned the nickname "the Shoe Fetish Slayer" for two reasons: one, he developed a fascination (and, later, a sexual attraction) to shoes after finding a pair of women's high heels in a junkyard at age five. Two, he chose at least two of his victims because he liked their shoes and cut off one victim's foot to use as a model for his shoe collection.

Brudos' shoe fetish may have shaped some of his murderous choices but it wasn't the cause. He had a history of violence beginning in adolescence and spent some time in a psychiatric hospital after threatening a woman with a knife and taking photos of her after forcing her to undress. He stole underwear from women's homes and raped at least one woman before progressing to murder. And, after his murders began, he engaged in other deviant sexual practices, including necrophilia and collecting body parts as trophies.

30. Has a Serial Killer Ever Committed Suicide? Suicide among serial killers is rare but it does happen. A 2012 study looked at 483 serial killers and found that 6.2 percent—about thirty—had taken their lives, most often after being captured. Israel Keyes, an Alaskan serial killer whose victim count the FBI is still trying to tally, is an example. Based on the eleven skulls he drew in prison in his own blood before he committed suicide in the Anchorage Correctional Complex in December 2012, they believe he has killed eleven people between 2001 and 2012.

Keyes had been arrested for the rape and murder of 18-year-old Samantha Koenig,whom he abducted from a local coffee stand. Two other victims have been identified. Keyes left "murder kits" buried in various locations around the country that contained, among other items, weapons and cash and, when he decided to kill, chose his victims randomly. ***Anyone with information concerning Keyes is encouraged to contact the FBI at 1-800-CALL-FBI.***

31. Are Most Serial Killers Insane? What do you do when the evidence against you is so overwhelming that you *know* you are going to be found guilty? What if, on top of that, your crimes are so heinous that the death penalty is staring you right in the face? For some serial killers, the choice is obvious; you plead Not Guilty by Reason of Insanity.

Several serial killers have traveled down this road: Albert Fish (serial killer, rapist, and cannibal executed for three murders between 1934 and 1932), John Wayne Gacy, Ken Bianchi to name a few. In fact, serial killers are more likely to plead Not Guilty by Reason of Insanity than other criminals (17 percent versus 1 percent). But they are much less likely to be successful (3 percent versus 25 percent).

There are several reasons for this. Serial murder typically involves a significant degree of planning as well as concerted efforts to evade detection; neither of these are congruent with a person who is so psychiatrically impaired that he either doesn't understand that what he is doing is wrong (so why cover it up?) or couldn't control his behavior (so why was he able to plan the crime)? And then there's the fact that jurors don't look favorably on defendants who hurt strangers—especially children. After his guilty verdict, a number of jurors stated that they actually believed Albert Fish *was* insane but were so disgusted by his rape and murder of three young children they wanted him executed anyway.

Herbert Mullin: Offering Human Sacrifices to Prevent a Major Earthquake

There is no question that Herbert Mullin, who killed thirteen random people in California over a two-year period, was seriously mentally ill long before he committed his first murder in 1972. Three years earlier, he had voluntarily committed himself to Mendocino State Hospital in California. There, he was diagnosed with schizophrenia aggravated by drug use and treated with antipsychotic medication. He routinely engaged in bizarre behavior that was observed by just about everyone who knew him: his former manager at a Goodwill store, his family, his friends. He was involuntarily committed to a psychiatric hospital in October 1969 and hospitalized again in 1970.

By May 1971, he was still using drugs, not taking his psychiatric medication, and began to believe that the voices he was hearing were telepathically communicated. After discovering that he and Albert Einstein shared a birthday, he also came to believe that this meant that he, too, was destined for great work. Unfortunately, by September 1972, he decided that his "great work" was to save California from a catastrophic earthquake, and that this job required human sacrifices.

Between October 1972 and February 1973, Mullin murdered ten people. Initially found incompetent to stand trial, he was convicted of ten murders. So far, he has been denied parole at least ten times; he will be eligible again in 2025. While several serial killers have tried to fake mental illness in order to plead Not Guilty by Reason of Insanity, Herbert Mullin was the real deal. A colleague of mine, Dr. Kris Mohandie, interviewed Mr. Mullin years after he was convicted and said that the inmate still wonders if his actions prevented a natural disaster. Oddly enough, on February 21, 1973 and eight days after he was arrested, a 5.9-magnitude earthquake struck Ventura County in southern California.

32. What are the Demographics of Healthcare Serial Killers? Between 1970 and 2018, there have been ninety convictions of healthcare serial killers worldwide. When you consider the number of healthcare professionals who report to work each day, that's an incredibly small number (less than one serial killer per two million professionals). But what they lack in numbers, they make up in volume; many of them operate undetected for years and leave quite a trail of bodies behind them; the number of suspicious deaths linked to those convicted is over 2,600. Who would be suspicious of a patient's death when they're already dying?

When we first discovered that a very small subset of medical professionals was prematurely assisting their patients' departure into the afterlife, most people thought it was the result of an overly zealous but well-intentioned attempt to relieve the patient's suffering. A closer look, though, quickly revealed that many of the patients were not in severe pain and were not at death's door. Hence, the "Angel of Mercy" became the "Angel of Death."

As far as who these "angels" are, 86 percent of the perpetrators were nurses, half men and half women. Twelve percent were doctors, and two percent an assortment of other medical professionals. Seventy percent of the deaths occurred in the hospital and twenty percent were in nursing homes. Even among an already vulnerable population—those receiving treatment for a physical illness—perpetrators tended to single out the most vulnerable: the critically ill, elderly, mentally compromised, and infants were over-represented among victims. The most common murder method was injection, either too much of what the patient was prescribed or something else (such as insulin or opiates).

33. Who Was the First Healthcare Professional to Become a Serial Killer? While we don't know for sure, Jane Toppan was one of the first ones identified and her case received a huge amount of attention at the time. Born Honora Kelly on March 31, 1854, she was arrested in 1901 and confessed to killing thirty-one people between 1895 and 1901. Victims included family, hospital patients, her landlord, friends, and a love rival. She appeared to have a wide range of motives; curiosity (she experimented with different medications and doses to see what would happen), revenge (on her foster sister, whom she thought was treated more favorably and had a better life), convenience (to get a job) and pleasure (she claimed to get a sexual thrill out of watching the light die out of her patient's eyes). Apparently, she even made herself sick to get sympathy from some of the men she dated.

As you can imagine, after she was arrested, medical professionals scrambled to figure out what was wrong with Jane. Surely, they reasoned, she must be "crazy;" why else would she kill all of those people? But she didn't *act* like it; everyone who evaluated her agreed that she was a smart woman who seemed to be mentally and physically normal. At a loss, experts eventually decided that, in spite of Toppan's normal appearance, she must be mad; they diagnosed her with "moral insanity," she successfully pleaded Not Guilty by Reason of Insanity, and she spent the last thirty-six years of her life in an institute for the criminally insane.

Today, Toppan would undoubtedly have been found guilty. Moral insanity back then was today's equivalent of "psychopathy" and it is no defense against murder. Toppan, herself, seemed puzzled by her "insanity" diagnosis, well aware that she was in touch with reality and did not have the serious mental illnesses that, back then, were recognized although not understood as psychosis. She was also aware that she was unable to experience emotions that others seemed to feel and understand. In 1904, she was interviewed in the asylum that was now her home and attempted to explain herself: "I do not know the feeling of fear, and I do not know the feeling of remorse, although I understand perfectly what these words mean. I do not seem to be able to realise the awfulness of the things I have done, although I realise what those awful things are. I seem incapable of realising the awfulness of it. Why don't I feel sorry, and grieve over it? I don't know.

34. Do Serial Killer Doctors and Serial Killer Nurses Have the Same Motives? There is some overlap but also some interesting differences. Serial killers from different healthcare professions often have different motives because they are at different levels on the medical totem pole. Doctors, for instance, sometimes kill from a sense of godlike power ("I get to decide whose life is worth living") or out of an experimental curiosity ("I wonder what would happen if I mixed these two drugs)." Joseph Michael Swango, convicted of four murders and suspected of up to sixty more between 1981 and 1987, apparently murdered patients for the pure joy of it. Excerpts from his diary at trial showed someone who, from an early age, was fascinated by death and dying and collected pictures of gruesome car accidents and macabre crimes.

For Swango, murder was especially thrilling; in fact, he wrote that his murders were"the only way I have of reminding myself that I'm still alive." Not only did he kill while he was on-duty, Swango was observed on at least one occasion sitting on a radiator beside a patient's bed, watching his patient deteriorate and die from what later turned out to be one of Swango's murders.

British doctor Harold Shipman is also believed to have enjoyed "playing God" with his elderly patients, but he also liked their money. In fact, two hundred and fifty patient deaths (1975-1998) didn't appear to arouse suspicion as quickly as Shipman's greed did. He was finally brought to justice after forging a patient's will and her lawyer-daughter began investigating. He isn't the only serial killer doctor driven by dollar signs; in the late nineteenth century, hotel owner and doctor, H.H. Holmes, murdered his victims (he confessed to twenty-seven) primarily for insurance money (he would take out policies on his hotel employees) and rob and murder wealthy hotel patrons and guests.

On other hand, serial killer nurses and other medical professionals, who are responsible for most of the direct patient care, may kill out of anger or frustration—to relieve tension from a personal crisis, to get "payback" against an unappreciative or abusive physician, to get rid of a "difficult" patient, or to reduce a burdensome workload. For example, nurse Orville Lynn Majors, responsible for the deaths of six patients between 1993 and 1995, apparently chose his victims based on how demanding or complaining they were. And Efren Saldivar, a respiratory therapist who killed at least six patients (and once confessed to murdering two hundred) at a Glendale, California hospital between 1988 and 1998, said his murders were prompted by too little staff and too many patients; "I'd look at the patient board and think, 'Who do we gotta get rid of?'"

However, one common theme seems to pop up in both doctors and nurses; the desire to be a "hero." Some perpetrators create medical crises to impress their colleagues with their resuscitation prowess. French doctor Frederic Pechier is currently awaiting trial for the murder of nine patients (and twenty-four poisonings) between 2008 and 2017. Many of them were his colleagues' patients undergoing mild medical procedures. Pechier reportedly poisoned their infusion bags in order to humiliate his fellow doctors and then save the day. Similarly, Kristen Gilbert, who murdered at least four VA patients in 1995 and 1996, injected her patients with epinephrine so her hospital-security-guard lover could watch her swoop in and bring them back to life. In these cases, the thrill is in the crisis and the death, from the eyes of the murderer, is an unfortunate but acceptable risk.

Niels Högel and the Rush

Niels Högel, a 42-year-old former German nurse, was jailed for life for the murder of eighty-five patients between the ages of thirty-four and ninety-six in his care. His recent convictions are for murders that occurred between 2000 and 2005 at two hospitals in northern Germany; he is already serving a life sentence for six murders between 2008 and 2015. Högel was originally caught in June 2005 when a nurse saw that a previously stable patient had developed an irregular heartbeat. He was already in the room when the patient had to be resuscitated and the nurse found empty medication containers in a trash can.

Högel admitted to giving various non-prescribed drugs that caused heart failure or circulatory collapse to his victims, in an attempt to show off his resuscitation skills to colleagues and fight off boredom. Two female nurses-in-training recall him asking to watch one of his rescue attempts, apparently in an attempt to impress them. (Sound familiar? While the two never met, Högel had a kindred spirit in American V.A. nurse Kristen Gilbert).

For years, Högel exhibited no red flags. Former classmates, teachers, and friends described him as "friendly," "fun" and "helpful," and were stunned by the charges against him. He apparently came from a loving and stable home; his father was a nurse. Not a single person in his life suspected that he secretly felt overwhelmed by his job and had begun drinking heavily.

During his confessions, he described at length the rush he got from creating his life-and-death emergencies. He said he felt euphoric when he managed to bring a patient back to life and devastated when he failed; this devastation would last a few days and then the urge to do it again would take over. A personality assessment after his arrest noted that he failed to see his patients as "individuals." Another report identified a "severe narcissistic disorder." Whatever the demons that drove him, Högel is Germany's deadliest postwar serial killer.

35. How Are Healthcare Serial Killers Caught? Perhaps not surprisingly, work colleagues are often the first to spot a deadly doctor or nurse. They notice that a colleague "predicts" when certain patients will die. They catch a nurse coming out of an unassigned patient's room or trying to prevent others from checking on their assigned patients. They find themselves wondering why there are so many "codes" or deaths when a certain person is on duty (most often on the night shift).

Sometimes, it's the physical evidence that kicks off an investigation: drugs are missing from a dispensary, toxicology results from a patient's unexpected death reveal toxic levels of a prescribed medication or the presence of an unprescribed one. Or a routine quality-assurance check shows a spike in patient deaths on a certain floor or during certain times.

After Canadian nurse Elizabeth Wettlaufer confessed to murdering eight patients between 2006 and 2017 at an Ontario nursing home, a massive public inquiry was conducted to find out why she was able to kill over such a long period and why, in the report's own words, "her killings would not have come to light had she not confessed." Among the findings was a lack of detailed tracking of patient deaths, a reluctance to disclose concerning information about a former nurse or doctor during employer reference checks, and a tendency to minimize or dismiss concerns reported by work colleagues.

36. Are Some Cult Leaders Also Serial Killers? There have been many malignant cult leaders who were responsible for the death of dozens, although many of them don't like to get their own hands dirty. Just think of Charles Manson or Ervil LeBaron (leader of a polygamist Mormon offshoot who used religious doctrine to justify his ordering of at least twenty-five murders between 1974 and 1981). Both persuaded (or ordered) followers to kill numerous innocent people. In addition to their homicidal proclivities, destructive cult leaders also share quite a few personality traits with serial killers—narcissism, superficial charm, manipulative, deceptive, controlling, and exploitive.

Are Serial Murderers More Likely to Be Atheists?

Why do atheists get such a bad rap? It's not clear but it's true. Popular opinion consistently puts "evil" and "atheist" in the same category, especially in comparison to our Bible-thumping neighbors. Not only are we likely to believe people of faith are more virtuous, we tend to make all kinds of erroneous assumptions about nonreligious folks, none of them good, especially when the "atheist" label gets applied. An example: In 2017, a survey of over 3,000 participants from thirteen countries were asked whether a serial killer was likely to be either a teacher or a teacher who was also an atheist. Just adding "atheist" to one of two fictional but otherwise identical descriptions of serial killers resulted in most people judging the teacher/atheist as the likely perpetrator. Strangely, even the most secular participants rated atheists as more deviant.

There is no factual evidence to support these commonly held opinions. In reality, the relationship between religion and serial murder is all over the board. There are serial-killing agnostics, Jews, Muslims, Satan worshippers, Mormons, and born-again Christians. In fact, there is a long history of serial killers who touted their spiritual affiliation at the same time they were murdering people; Dennis "BTK" Rader (who strangled ten people between 1974 and 1991), was a Lutheran church deacon and president of his church council. John Wayne Gacy (who murdered thirty-three young men between 1972 and 1978) thought about becoming a priest. Gary Ridgway (convicted of murdering forty-nine sex workers between 1982 and 1998) was once a devout Baptist who went door to door witnessing to his neighbors. And Janie Lou Gibbs tithed $3,000 of the $30,000-plus inheritance she received after poisoning her husband, son, and three grandsons to the church.

37. Why Do Serial Killers Keep Trophies? For the same reasons anyone does; to remember. Contrary to popular opinion, all serial killers don't collect trophies to remind them of their victim. In fact, most of them don't. Only 24 percent of serial killers keep some sort of trophy. (Seven percent actually keep a diary.)

For some serial killers, keeping a memento—a lock of hair, jewelry, a driver's license—helps prolong, even nourish, the memory of the crime. It gives them a sense of ownership and accomplishment, a reminder of what they've done and a way to keep the memory alive. In a twisted way, it's similar to a middle-aged athlete who's always pulling out his high-school yearbook to relive his glory days.

Trophy-collecting among serial killers has traditionally been an all-male sport. But Romanian serial killer Axenia Varlan (aka Mara Varlane and, later, the "Ogress of Bukavina), may be the exception. Arrested in 1928, she allegedly collected various body parts of her nine victims (including ears and fingers) as souvenirs. What made this particularly gruesome was the fact that many of her victims were family members, including her four children, her parents, and her mother-in-law.

38. Why Do Some Serial Killers Exaggerate Their Body Count or Confess to Killings They Didn't Commit? Serial killers typically confess to other murders or exaggerate their body count only when they're already going down for life (or possibly) death. With nothing to lose, some serial killers want to enhance their infamy by being seen as more evil and more depraved; as their thinking goes, better to be feared than ignored.

Then, of course, there are the practical perks that false confessions can offer—free lunches, lots of attention through police interviews, and travel in fresh air and comfort while visiting body sites and police stations. In the 1980s, serial killer Henry Lee Lucas (convicted of killing three and suspected of eight more between 1960 and 1983) confessed to over six hundred murders—thrilling law enforcement and earning himself a lot of hamburgers and milkshakes and a certain celebrity status—before it became impossible to ignore the holes in his confession or the fact that DNA conclusively proved he was innocent of at least twenty murders he had confessed to.

The "Recovered Memories" of an Innocent Serial Killer

Since the 1990s, clinicians and researchers have debated recovered memories, how likely it is that they are real and under what condition they might genuinely occur. Both groups are in agreement, however, that three things have to be present in order for a memory to have been recovered; the event had to occur, the forgetting had to be real (as opposed to being kept a secret) and the spontaneous recovery must be spontaneous (as opposed to coerced).

Swedish citizen Sture Bergwall, a.k.a. Thomas Quick, a Swedish criminal who confessed to more than thirty murders while incarcerated in a Scandinavian psychiatric institute for personality disorders, was no angel. He was a bank robber and a convicted child molester. But his murderous career (he was convicted of eight murders, all of which were later overturned) appeared to have been inspired by a group of psychologists, therapists, and psychiatrists, who cheered on his every confession, and backed by a group of law enforcement professionals willing to overlook discrepancies in his accounts (including the fact that two of his alleged victims were alive and well). All of his convictions were eventually overturned and he was released in 2013.

39. Do Most Serial Killers Have a Criminal History Before They Begin Killing? Most don't have a *violent* criminal history before they start murdering. However, most do have some criminal convictions or at least multiple contacts with police before they're arrested for their first violent crime. A look at ten male serial killers with the highest body counts from the 1970s through the 1990s, for instance, found that four of them had no felony convictions, three had nonviolent criminal histories (vandalism, theft, public indecency) and three had more serious convictions (sexual assault toward a minor, kidnapping, child molestation).

Depending on the motive, the pre-killing criminal history varies; sexually motivated serial killers may have previous charges for voyeurism or burglary while I've noticed that financially motivated serial killers (especially women) have more than their share of fraud, check forgery, or other money-motivated convictions. Substance-abuse charges (possession of a controlled substance, public intoxication) are not common.

There is a subset of serial killers whose kills are an extension of a well-established pattern of violent behavior including rape, assault, domestic violence, and so forth. Almost 20 percent of the serial killers in the Radford/FGCU database (a collection of over 5,000 U.S. and international serial killers) had killed, gone to prison, and had been released and killed again. With longer prison sentences and reductions in parole, those folks are not going to be back on the streets to kill again.

Released to Kill Again

If there ever was an argument for long prison sentences, Scottish serial killer Angus Sinclair would be it. In 1961, at age sixteen, he raped and strangled to death his seven-year old neighbor, Catherine Reehill. He was released just six years later and, in 1977, six women disappeared. In 1982, he received a life sentence after admitting to eleven rapes and indecent assault. However, twenty years later, DNA linked him to a 1978 Glasgow murder and that led to three more victims. He was ultimately convicted of the murder of four women (and suspected in the murder of four more).

40. What are Serial Killers' Most Common Occupations? Think of a job and there's probably a serial killer who's worked it. There have been serial killer doctors, law students, border patrollers, construction workers, fast-food managers, housewives, grave diggers, and college professors. That being said, there *are* certain professions that tend to be more popular among serial killers, because either the job is short-term/transient (general laborer, warehouse manager), or because they make it easier to get access to potential victims (long-haul truck driver, military, or police/security officer).

It was once proposed that many serial killers had military experience and that their military training and combat experience has reinforced the violence and aggression that they then applied to their victims. It turns out that just over twenty percent of serial killers were in the military at some point in their lives. While under 10 percent of U.S. adults are veterans today, eighteen percent were veterans back in the 1980s (when many of today's infamous murderers were active). So, while there might be a *slight* overrepresentation of serial killing veterans, the military certainly wasn't the serial-killing training grounds once hypothesized.

Professional Wrestler and Serial Killer

While there have been a number of unusual professions occupied by serial killers, professional wrestler would surely make the top five, especially since she was a female. Juana Barraza was, at one time, a hit on the Mexican *Lucha Libre* masked-wrestling circuit for her role as "The Lady of Silence (La Matavietas)." Born December 27, 1957, Juana was a late bloomer as far as serial killers go; she didn't kill her first victim until she was in her early forties, injured her back, and was unable to continue wrestling.

But when she started, Barraza never slowed down. While the exact date of her first murder is unclear, it likely occurred around 1998. She quickly developed a common way of operating; she targeted old ladies whom she strangled and then robbed, often of small or inexpensive items. She typically gained entry into her victim's houses by pretending to help them in some way—carry their groceries for them, help them get social services, give them a medical checkup, and so forth. The police estimate that she killed between forty-two and forty-six women. (One reason Juana was able to escape justice for so long was her large, somewhat masculine frame and law enforcement's refusal to believe a woman was a serial killer even after several eyewitnesses pointed to a female killer.)

Juana was arrested in 2006 after an elderly woman surprised a younger woman running from what turned out to be a dead body. She was convicted and sentenced to seven hundred and fifty-nine years for the murder of eleven elderly women.

41. Do Most Serial Killers Secretly Want to Get Caught?

Ummmm, no. I think the reason this idea has been thrown around is because of the silly ways that some serial killers have been captured—driving without a license plate, parking in front of a fire hydrant, signing a hotel registry in their actual name and then murdering someone in the hotel room, asking law enforcement if they can trace a computer disk, etc. I think a better explanation for these rookie mistakes (and none of these killers were rookies) is that, as a serial killer's body count grows, they are more likely to become overly confident and think they *can't* be caught. Their guard comes down and the next thing they know, they're sitting in a jail cell.

42. Has a Serial Killer Ever Stopped Killing on His Own?

The short answer is yes. We know there have been unsolved murders that have suddenly stopped. But we don't know why. There can be a lot of reasons why serial killing would stop. Did the killer move away from his original target zone? Is he in jail for something else? Has he aged out? Or was he sidelined by medical problems? Even the most prolific criminal tends to wear out as he gets older; we rarely see an active serial killer who is older than fifty.

There are also psychological reasons why a serial killer slows down or stops, although remorse is not usually one of them. Maybe he has a close call and decides to cool it for a while or wises up about the perils of DNA. Sometimes a new job or new relationship serves as a stabilizing force. A 2008 report on serial murder for the FBI's National Center for the Analysis of Violent Crime also found that killers may quiet down when they find other outlets for their emotions. And a number of killers, including Samuel Little and Dennis Rader, reported substituting sexual activities, such as autoerotic asphyxiation, in between, or as a substitute for violent sex.

And yes, there have even been a few serial killers who turned themselves in, such as Wayne Adam Ford (murdered four women between 1997 and 1998), keeping female body parts as trophies) and Edmund Kemper (killed ten people, including his grandparents and mother between 1964 and 1973). Ford had reached out to his brother, Rodney, the night before he walked into a sheriff's station, upset and telling his sibling that he had "hurt some people" and needed help; Rodney went with him to see the sheriff and encouraged him to confess. When Kemper was asked why he confessed, he stated something to the effect that there was no reason to kill anyone else after he killed his mother (who psychiatrists had long thought was the symbolic target behind his other murders) as killing anyone else "wasn't serving any physical or real or emotional purpose."

43. Do Serial Killers Study Other Serial Killers? Some serial killers not only study the "mentors" who have gone before them, but also the law-enforcement strategies that captured them. Alaskan serial killer Israel Keyes was a big fan of Ted Bundy and tried hard to avoid Bundy's mistakes. For example, he thought one of Bundy's weaknesses was the fact that he preferred a certain type of victim; Keyes went after men, women, couples, even children. He was determined to have no victim profile. He also read books by criminal profilers, taking detailed notes so he could avoid behaviors that could predict his personality or might point to his identify.

44. Do Serial Killers Ever Express Remorse? The only remorse that most murderers feel is remorse over getting caught. There are rare exceptions, though, and serial killer Mack Ray Edwards may be one. In 1970, he and a partner entered a home and abducted three girls. Two got away but the third was still missing. Before the police had even started looking for her, Edwards entered the Los Angeles Police Department, described the kidnapping, and gave directions to the missing girl, who was found unharmed.

He also told them that, for the previous seventeen years, he had been killing children: an eight-year-old girl in 1953, two kids in a single day in 1956, two 16-year old boys in 1968, and a 13-year-old in 1969. He described desperately trying to control his compulsion to kill for years but had finally realized the urge was too strong so he decided to turn himself in. He attempted suicide twice while waiting for his trial. During his trial, he told the jury he wanted the death penalty, a wish they happily granted. However, when the appeals process continued to drag on without his consent, he finally succeeded in taking his own life.

Is There Some Good in Everybody—Even a Serial Killer?

There is no way a person who has taken the lives of innocent people can ever make up for what they have done. And there are many who argue that no one should be given that chance. So, in 1987, when a story broke that revealed that serial killer Edmund Kemper, convicted of killing six female college students and four others in California between 1964 and 1973, was the voice behind numerous popular audiobooks, reactions ranged from horror to outrage.

The story is true but a little more complicated. His narrating work came about as a result of a nonprofit partnership between inmates at the California Department of Corrections and Rehabilitations California Medical Facility (CMC) and the Blind Project; the goal is to provide materials for the blind and visually impaired (the audiobooks are not distributed to the general public) while providing inmates with the opportunity to do something worthwhile. Kemper suffered a stroke in 2015 and, as such, is no longer involved with the project; however, he spent over 5,000 hours recording for the visually impaired and, at times, worked up to eight hours a day. By some accounts, he produced more books than any other inmate.

But why? Did Kemper get some kind of perverse pleasure knowing thousands of people would unknowingly be mesmerized by the voice of a serial killer? Was he so bored in prison that anything was better than staring at the walls of his prison cell? Was there a part of Kemper that found satisfaction in enriching other people's lives? He's the only one who knows.

45. Has a Serial Killer Ever Been Rehabilitated? Well, theoretically, yes, although it depends on what you mean. There have been serial killers who have been released and never killed again. Karla Homolka, who cut a sweet deal with prosecutors before video evidence made it abundantly clear that she played an active role in the sexual serial murders committed by her and her husband, Paul Bernardo, was released in 2005 after serving twelve years. She married the brother of her criminal defense attorney, has three children, and, as far as anyone knows, has remained crime-free.

In the U.K., 10-year-old Mary Bell, serially killed two young boys, ages three and four. She spent twelve years in psychiatric care and was released in 1980. She was twenty-three. Four years later, she had a daughter, who was unaware of her mother's past until they were both tracked down by reporters. Today, Mary Bell, who lives under an assumed name, is sixty years old, a grandmother, and has had no more run-ins with the law.

However, there are far more examples of serial killers who everyone thought was safe and proved everyone wrong. Kenneth McDuff was arrested and given three life sentences for the 1966 murders of two teenage boys and the rape and murder of a 16-year old girl. Instead, through a series of unfortunate events, he was paroled in 1989. Three days after he was released, he began killing prostitutes. He was executed in 1998.

Another infamous example was Arthur Shawcross, also known as the Genesee River Killer. Arthur was first convicted of the 1972 rape and murder of a young boy and girl in his hometown of Rochester, New York; through a plea deal, he was only convicted of manslaughter. He was paroled for good behavior in 1987, at which time he promptly began killing again, this time focusing on sex workers in upstate New York. He ended up killing twelve people in the two years following his release and was rearrested in 1989. He died in custody in 2008.

While most murderers only kill once, serial-killer researcher, Mike Aamodt, found that, out of 2,883 serial killers from his database, six hundred and fifty (22 percent) killed again after they had been released from prison after an initial murder conviction. The majority of them (73.5 percent) were still on parole.

"Don't Make Serial Killers Roomies in Prison"

This 2012 *National Post* headline would be funny if the story didn't have such a tragic ending. In November 2010, serial killer Michael Wayne McGray murdered a fellow inmate, 33-year-old Jeremy Phillips. McGray had already left a trail of blood behind him; he had previously been convicted of six murders and was suspected in up to sixteen.

At the time of the murder, Phillips and McGray were bunkmates at a medium-security prison in Canada; McGray had transferred from a maximum yard earlier. Other inmates said that Phillips had been nervous about McGray but custody officers thought everyone would be safe. McGray confessed within twenty-four hours of the murder, describing himself as a psychopath and stating that he tied up Phillips with strips of a torn bedsheet, shoved a sock down his mouth, and strangled him. Afterward, he allegedly told investigators that the murder had been just been a matter of time due to "his mental-health issues that stirred fantasies of stacking bodies."

An internal investigation revealed that McGray had applied for the lower-security transfer but had warned prison officials against giving him a cellmate; in fact, on two previous occasions, he had turned down a transfer when told he would have to double up with another inmate. He was on a single-cell waitlist at the time of the murder. Not surprisingly, it also made the recommendation that serial murderers might do better in a cell of their own.

46. How Smart Are Serial Killers? Not as smart as you probably think. One of the biggest myths about serial killers is that they are evil geniuses who manage to evade law enforcement for years due to their cunning enterprise and superior IQ. That may be true for a subset of serial killers but it's certainly not the norm.

Only two percent of people have an IQ score above 132. Among those serial killers whose IQ give some merit to the "evil genius" myth are: Unabomber Ted Kaczynski (IQ of 167); Charlene Gallego, who with her husband Gerald murdered ten women between 1978 and 1980 and had a reported IQ of 160; and Dating Game Killer Rodney Alcala, who was convicted of the murder of seven women between 1971 and 1979, and suspected of killing many more. As a contestant on *The Dating Game* (hence, the moniker), Alcala used his moderately gifted IQ of 135 and superficial charm to win the bachelorette's heart, only to lose it when she met him in person and realized how creepy he was in person.

On the whole, though, serial killers are not particularly bright, having an average IQ of 93-94. Given that 51.6 percent of all Americans fall somewhere between 90 and 110 (with 100 being the average), that's nothing to brag about. In fact, if you were to plot out all of the known IQs of serial killers and put a dart at the halfway point, meaning 50 percent of the IQs were to the right of the dart and the other half were to the left, the dart would be at 85. This indicates that more serial killers have a lower-than-average IQ than those who are gifted. Gary Ridgway, for example, had an IQ of 81 of but still managed to get away with the murders of over fifty women.

However, this average is somewhat misleading. In the "normal" population, only 2.2 percent of us fall at the outer edges of intelligence. When it comes to serial killers, though, you are much more likely to find extremes at either end; 10.6 percent of serial killers have an IQ above 130 and a whopping 15.2 percent fall below 70.

Who is Smart Enough to be Executed?

In 2002, the U.S. Supreme Court ruled that it was cruel and unusual punishment for inmates with intellectual disabilities to be executed. So, what does that mean for intellectually limited serial killers? Are they able to avoid the Grim Reaper?

Not usually. Gary Ray Bowles, convicted of killing six men in 1994, was executed in 2019. Prior to his death, he argued that he was intellectually disabled, as evidenced by two intelligence-test scores that were subpar (74 and 80), affidavits from several psychologists whose opinion supported Bowles' argument, and statements from people who knew him when he was young that suggested he had intellectual difficulties. Obviously, none of the ploys worked.

It also didn't work for Alfredo Prieto, a serial killer who was convicted of murdering three people and raping two between 1988 and 1990 (although never tried, his DNA also linked him to another six murders). After being sentenced to death in Virginia, Prieto argued that his IQ test scores of 66 and 73 made him ineligible for execution; at that time, Virginia used 70 as a general cutoff for establishing mental retardation. However, other factors came into consideration, not the least of which was the fact that Prieto had performed well at a Los Angeles high school after moving to California from El Salvador and not speaking a word of English. It was also noted that he had demonstrated sophisticated criminal tactics (leaving little evidence and, at one point, stealing and using his girlfriend's brothers' identification) and, while in prison, filing a series of handwritten lawsuits about the rights on inmates that were actually successful. He was executed on October 1, 2015.

Debra Denice Brown had more luck. She and her partner in crime, Alton Coleman, were responsible for the death of eight men, women, and children between May and July of 1984. Both were sentenced to death and Coleman, who with an IQ of 72 was no rocket scientist himself, was executed in 2002. In 2018, Brown's death sentence was commuted to life in prison and Indiana's only female death-row inmate was moved. The Indiana

Attorney General's Office cited an IQ score of 59 she had obtained at age twelve (as an adult she scored a 74) in conjunction with the master-slave relationship she had with Coleman, which included severe physical abuse and her dependent personality disorder, as deciding factors in the sentence change.

Are you wondering if a serial killer has ever "played dumb" in an effort to avoid execution? We don't know for sure but I'm betting on yes. Derrick Todd Lee, who murdered seven Baton Rouge-area women between 1992 and 2003, scored a 65 on an IQ test during his trial but as high as 91 as a child. While some variability between tests is expected, a twenty-six-point difference in the absence of a head injury or illness suggests something other than aptitude.

47. Do Serial Killers Become Addicted to Killing? Some serial killers do seem to become somewhat addicted to murder. Just like we see substance abusers needing to take and more of a drug to get satisfied over time, *sexual* serial killers in particular seem to escalate. Most serial killers start out with smaller crimes, such as voyeurism or theft. When they begin killing, the times in between murders often become shorter and sometimes the violence becomes more extreme.

This is also true for some thrill serial killers. However, just because some serial killers have an urge or a compulsion to kill doesn't mean they can't control it when the risks outweigh the rewards. I've yet to meet a serial killer who murdered in broad daylight, standing in front of a police station.

For other serial killers, murder almost becomes a problem-solving strategy, i.e., *If I have poisoned my wife and gotten away with it, it becomes an easier choice with the next spouse*. Perhaps this is why some serial killers kill different people for different reasons; Sofia Zhukova, for example, an alleged Russian serial killer currently on trial for murdering three people between 2005 and 2013, is accused of murdering a tenant after he allegedly raped her, an elderly friend in order to steal her money, and a child whom she thought was too noisy and threw ice cream at her after Zhukova told her to quiet down. Clearly, she had decided that there was one solution to any problem.

48. Does Serial Murder Ever Become a Hobby? This sounds like an insulting question and I am no means trivializing the horror of serial killing. Here's where this question comes from: if you look at studies in leisure science, (yes, there really is such a thing), leisure is defined as the choice of an activity that gives pleasure or a challenge in one's free time. At its core, leisure is about personal satisfaction and choice: you do it because you want to, not because you have to. Some criminologists and a few leisure scientists have noticed that some crimes are, in and of themselves, deviant leisure activities (defacing public buildings with graffiti, for example) and that some such activities (consumption of violent pornography, for example) might lead to crime.

They've also noticed that some serial killers tend to approach their murders like some hobbyists approach a hobby; they carefully search for the right victim, they plan the abduction, they keep mementos. One recent study analyzed a large number of serial homicide cases and found that serial murders often used "leisure-related themes" when describing their murderous activities, i.e., describing serial murder as a game, talking about the thrills and intense sensations that accompanied the kill, and describing each murder as a unique, personal project or celebration. Dennis Rader (the Bind-Torture-Murder killer responsible for the deaths of ten between 1974 and 1991), for example, compared killing to going fishing and claimed to have committed a murder to celebrate St. Patrick's Day. He kept journals and drew pictures of his murders and fantasies, researched other serial killers, and he even took bondage photos of himself in women's clothes.

The Serial Murder Game

While many serial killers have toyed with their victims and played games with the police, Russian serial killer Alexander Pichushkin actually aspired to a victim count that would match the number of squares (64) on a chessboard; chess was his favorite pastime. An indiscriminate killer, between 1992 and 2006 he lured men, women, and children into Moscow's Bitsa Park using a variety of lures—promise of vodka, offers to see his dog's grave, and so forth. He had a special fondness for murdering old men.

Once they walked to a remote location in the park, Pichushkin would kill them, usually by beating them to death with a hammer. His signature was sticking an empty vodka bottle into a hole his hammer had left in his victim's head. He was finally caught when his last victim told her son she was going to the park with Pichushkin and she disappeared.

When he was arrested, Pichushkin readily told the police all about his murderous exploits. He shared his diary with them as well as a special chessboard which had sixty squares filled in; Pichushkin said this was his victim count. Because only forty-nine bodies were recovered, this was the number he was convicted of, although Pichushkin urged authorities to include the other eleven victims. His confession to additional murders did not appear to arise from guilt or remorse; rather, he wanted to be sure he beat the serial killer he considered his "competitor"—Andrei Chikatilo, who, between 1978 and 1990, claimed fifty-three victims of his own.

which had sixty squares filled in. Pichushkin said this was his victim count. Because only forty-nine bodies were recovered, this was the number he was convicted of, although Pichushkin urged authorities to include the other eleven victims. His confession to additional murders did not appear to come from guilt or remorse; rather, he wanted to be sure he beat the serial killer he considered his "competitor"—Andrei Chikatilo, who, between 1978 and 1990, claimed fifty-three victims of his own.

Part 3: Female Serial Killers.

Would you be surprised to know that, during the first thirty years of the twentieth century, women made up 30 percent of all serial killers? Today, it's around 10 percent. But don't count lady killers out; what female serial killers lack in numbers, they make up in longevity. These quiet killers get away with their crimes twice as long as their male peers.

49. What Is the Typical Profile of a Female Serial Killer? When Aileen Wuornos, a prostitute with a horrific personal history of childhood abuse and a host of previously committed crimes under her belt, murdered seven men in 1989 and 1990, she was hailed as the first female serial killer even though there were women quietly bumping off spouses, children, neighbors, and acquaintances decades before Wuornos was born. The reason she was hailed as so unique was not because she committed so many murders, but because she did it in such a *masculine* way; she targeted strangers, she shot them to death, and her motives were a combination of revenge (for the way society had treated her) and robbery.

Here's a snapshot of the average U.S. female serial killer: in her twenties or thirties, middle-class, probably married, probably Christian, probably of average intelligence. She may work in a caregiving role, such as nurse, Sunday-school teacher, babysitter, or stay-at-home mom. She tends to be above-average in physical attractiveness, which helps her gain the trust of her victims. Sound like anyone you know? Perhaps your next-door neighbor?

A Mother-Daughter Serial-Killing Team

If you have a serial killer in your family, let's hope it's a man. That's because, while most male serial killers are out there stalking strangers, most female killers are plotting the demise of their loved ones. Take Rachel and Diane Staudte. In 2012 and 2013, mother Diane and favorite daughter Rachel systematically poisoned three other family members with antifreeze: 61-year-old husband Mark, 26-year-old brother Shaun, and 22-year-old sister Sarah.

Mark's and Shaun's death raised no alarms; however, when Sarah survived and was admitted to the hospital, Diane's odd behavior (laughing and joking when her daughter was on death's door), Sarah's mysterious symptoms, and an anonymous tip (from Diane's minister) suggesting foul play led to a police investigation and eventual confessions. Police were amazed at the trivial motives given, such as Shaun's annoying behavior or Sarah's reluctance to get a job. They were chilled to learn that, had Diane and Rachel not been arrested, their next target was Diane's 12-year-old daughter.

50. How Many Female Serial Killers Have There Been? In his 2007 book, *Female Serial Killers: How and Why Women Become Monsters*, author Peter Vronsky lists one hundred and forty documented female serial killers. Serial-killer researcher Mike Aamodt estimates there have been five hundred and fourteen since 1910. A website called Unknown Misandry, whose sole purpose appears to be to document female wickedness (particularly against men), cites more than nine hundred and eighty; some of these could not be verified or the person was accused but never charged or convicted. The truth is probably somewhere in between.

Regardless of the actual number, women are much less likely to commit serial murder than men; 16-17 percent of serial killers are female. Here's an interesting fact, though: Men commit 90 percent of *all* murders, leaving only 10 percent of all one-time murders for the fairer sex. That means that, statistically speaking, women commit a higher percentage of serial murders than other types of homicides.

51. Why Do Female Serial Killers Kill? While there have been numerous attempts to sort male serial killers by their motives, there has only been one such attempt to do the same with female serial killers. Here's what they came up with:

- **Black widows**. These women kill multiple spouses or lovers, typically for money. Real-life examples include Blanche Taylor Moore (convicted of murdering one husband via with arsenic poisoning and attempting to poison a boyfriend between 1968 and 1989) and Melissa Ann Shephard Weeks (convicted of murdering her second husband in 1991, suspected of killing her third husband in 2001, and attempted murder of her fourth husband in 2012).

- **Angels of death**. These are lethal caretakers who typically poison or suffocate vulnerable patients in a hospital or nursing home. Their motive is often a sense of power or control although some of these killers say they have murdered to relieve tension. Another kind of "angel of death" is the serial killer who murders for attention or sympathy; this includes the "hero" nurse who creates a medical emergency and then impresses others with her resuscitative skills (unless she fails and the patient dies) or the mother who induces or fakes illness in her children to get sympathy and praise for her long-suffering devotion to a sick or special needs child; death is typically either a result of overly zealous illness induction (for example, cutting off the air of a child to induce a medical crisis via apnea, but the child dies). Examples include English nurse Beverly Allitt (a nurse, she murdered four infants in 1991) and Marybeth Tinning (although she was only convicted of the 1985 death of her four-month-old daughter, she is suspected of killing all nine of her children, none of whom lived past age four).

- **Profit killers**. These serial killers target acquaintances, family members, or strangers as a way to make a living. An infamous example included Dorothea Puente, who lured vulnerable tenants to her boarding home and killed them for insurance money. Between 1982 and 1988, she killed at least nine and is suspected of up to fifteen.
- **Team killers**. Two or more people who serially kill together. The motive is typically determined by the dominant partner and could range from sexual sadism to thrills to money. Between 1999 and 2005, "business partners" Olga Rutterschmidt and Helen Golay collected over $2.8 million by purchasing insurance policies on homeless men, taking care of the beneficiaries until the policies were active, and then killing them. In contrast, Ian Brady and Myra Hindley, Gerald and Charlene Gallego, and Alvin and Judith Ann Neelley bonded over sexual depravity.
- **Revenge-seekers**. These serial killers kill people close to the target of the revenge, often children.

Martha Johnson had the nasty habit of rolling on top of, and smothering, one of her children after a particularly bad fight with her husband. Between 1977 and 1982, she killed four of them.

Example of a Revenge-Seeker

In 2019, 26-year old Brittany Pilkington was sentenced to thirty-seven years in prison after confessing that she murdered her three sons (ages three months and four years) between 2014 and 2015 because she was jealous of the preferential treatment her husband gave them over her and the couple's three-year-old daughter. The prosecution agreed to take the death penalty off the table when it was revealed that she was intellectually disabled (IQ of 71) and her husband, 43-year-old Joseph Pilkington, had once been her mother's boyfriend and had pleaded guilty to having sex with her as a minor in 2016.

- **Sexual predator**. Sexual sadism or another deviant sexual interest is the motivator. Aileen Wuornos (convicted of killing six men between November of 1989 and November of 1990) is the only solo female serial killer typically placed in this category, primarily because her kills took place when she was engaging in sex work and she targeted her clients. However, I think putting her in this category is inaccurate; there is no evidence that she obtained sexual pleasure during her murders and she herself cited money (she robbed her victims) and revenge on society as her primary motives. Genuine female sexual serial killers are more likely to be women who have hooked up with a sexually sadistic male and join in their brutal activities.

Female serial killers, like their male counterparts, also don't fit neatly into categories or types, particularly when it comes to motives. In fact, a recent study suggests that trying to classify female serial killers by motives might not be particularly useful, as many of them have more than one. Instead, it might be better to differentiate them by the nature of their relationships with the victims and how they are targeted. The "occupational" female serial murderer meets, targets, and gains access to her victims through her career, whereas the "hearthside" female serial murderer interacts and accesses victims through personal contact. Most female offenders don't kill from both groups, suggesting this might be a way to distinguish between them and, ultimately, better understand them.

Munchausen by Proxy Before There Was a Name for It

From 1946 to 1969, seven children died under the care of Martha Woods, including three of her biological children, a nephew and niece, a neighbor's child, and an adopted son. Several others narrowly escaped. Unfortunately, Woods was married to a military man and she and her husband moved all over the United States, making it much easier for her to fly under the radar. Of course, back then, who would have suspected Woods of murdering children anyway?

Here's how Woods typically operated. She would rush an unconscious baby to the emergency room, explaining that the child had suddenly stopped breathing. The baby would be thoroughly checked out and, after recovering, would be sent back into Woods' care, where the same thing would happen again. This happened twenty-seven times over twenty-three years. Not surprisingly, Woods was always alone with the child when the medical emergency happened.

Six of the seven murders were listed as natural deaths. Woods did come under police scrutiny but not in a way that would save anyone's life. Not only was Woods a serial killer, she was also a pathological liar who apparently needed constant attention. She complained that someone was trying to burn her house down. She insisted that someone was circling her house. After she and her husband adopted their first child, she told law enforcement officers that the child's biological parents had shown up on her doorstep and threatened her life if she didn't give them their child back.

Police patiently investigated each claim and found no merit to any of them; in fact, they found the biological parents peacefully living in another state. They later stated that, at the time, they suspected Woods had made it all up and privately thought she was a crackpot. They did not, however, suspect she was a murderer.

Martha Woods' luck finally ran out thanks to a courageous young doctor at Johns Hopkins Hospital, who was astonished to learn that both of her adopted children—7-month-old Paul and 2-year-old Judy—had been admitted to the hospital on multiple occasions with the same breathing problems.

On August 20, 1969, Paul was again admitted to Johns Hopkins; this time, though, he failed to respond to attempts to revive him, lapsed into a coma, and died a month later. Johns Hopkins called the police.

An investigation ensued and authorities finally discovered the pattern linking the deaths of all the other children. The evidence was so compelling that Woods was the only common denominator in each death that the judge allowed in evidence of these cases even though previous criminal behavior is almost always excluded in a trial. The judge's reasoning, upheld on appeal, was that the similarities in each of these cases could be used to prove a criminal "pattern" or "signature." Woods was convicted of first-degree murder and sentenced to life imprisonment.

I interviewed the attorney who prosecuted this case, Charles Bernstein, and he told me a chilling story he heard from Judy Woods' new adoptive mom following Martha Woods' conviction. While the Johns Hopkins doctors had been convinced of Woods' guilt, they were never certain as to how she had induced the cyanotic episodes that led to the children's medical crises and, in some cases, death. This story may have solved that mystery.

Mr. Bernstein said Judy's new mom told him that Judy, at that time around age four, was doing well but had done something upsetting recently. Judy was playing with her two-year-old sibling, who had a rattle that Judy wanted. Judy took it away from the toddler. When the toddler began to cry, the adoptive mom witnessed Judy reach over, pinch her nose closed, and put her other hand under the toddler's jaw so her mouth could not be opened. Mom quickly intervened and no harm was done. But Bernstein said this was exactly the way doctors had guessed Woods had harmed the babies in her care.

52. How Are Female Serial Killers Unlike Their Male Counterparts? The motives of male and female serial killers often differ, and this difference can drive crime scene behaviors. Female serial killers rarely, if ever, kill for sexual reasons (this is the second most common motive among male serial killers) unless they have hooked up with a man. Because sex is not a motive, they are much less likely to rape, mutilate, or torture their victims (at least in the same way; slowly poisoning someone to death and watching them suffer is certainly a form of torture). The most common motive of female serial killers is money, with power/attention a close second; as such, murder is more of a means to an end and they are likely to choose relatively quick ways of murder—poison, smothering, or, less commonly, shooting.

Also, female serial killers tend to kill people they know and kill them at home or in a familiar place, such as a hospital or day care, while male serial killers tend to go out hunting; in fact, 65 percent of males stalked their victims prior to killing them (in comparison to 5 to 20 percent of female serial killers *(depending on the study).

And don't forget: what female serial killers lack in numbers, they make up for in stealth and deception; in comparison to male serial killers, a female serial killer is likely to kill more victims and fly under the radar longer than her male peers. On average, female serial killers kill six victims before they are caught. Men average three to four.

Jollyamma Joseph's Murderous Approach to Life's Obstacles

For years, Jolly Joseph talked about how her house was cursed. Her mother-in-law died from a mysterious illness. At least three of her close relatives suffered fatal heart attacks, and her two-year-old niece choked to death on a piece of food. But by October 2019, Indian police had a different theory.

In October 2019, 47-year-old wife and mother Jollyamma "Jolly" Joseph was arrested for the murder of her first husband, Roy Thomas. The news stunned her neighbors, who described her as kind and welcoming, a good woman. Family members said she was a caring sister, a cherished daughter, and a bright student. It was not until her brother-in-law challenged the validity of his father's will that Indian law enforcement had ever heard of Joseph.

While it was the unwitnessed and unregistered will that Joseph produced that convinced her brother-in-law to contact law enforcement, perhaps it was the geographic distance between Joseph, residing in the Koodathayi village in the northern Kerali province of India, and her U.S.-based brother-in-law that kept him from falling for her charms and, as it turned out, deception. Others were not so lucky. What started out as a property dispute has morphed into a serial-killer investigation as Joseph has allegedly confessed to murdering six family members between 2002 and 2016—a mother-in-law, father-in-law, husband, uncle-in-law, cousin-in-law, and the 2-year-old daughter of her husband's cousin.

It turns out that, over the years, Joseph used murder to solve a number of her problems. Her motives for individual murders varied, although money appeared to be an overall theme. This was no woman living in desperate poverty, though. Several people have talked about Joseph's "extravagant" interest in living the high life. Police now suspect that the documents that emerged after the death of her in-laws, leaving Joseph and her husband their property, were false. Joseph's suspected murder of her unemployed husband also appears to be motivated by an attempt to get rid of someone whom she perceived as a financial burden and emotional strain; ironically, it was the emergence of a new will after her husband's death, leaving everything to Joseph, that first led her brother-in-law to the police.

Retaliation may have been another motive. Few people questioned the alleged "curse" that appeared to haunt Jollyamma Joseph's family. But when multiple family members began dying, Mathew Manjadiyii, Roy's uncle, was not so quick to accept Joseph's latest assertion that her husband had a heart attack. He insisted on a postmortem examination. Even after traces of cyanide were found in Roy's system, though, authorities believed Joseph's assertion that her husband had committed suicide due to financial woes. Who do you think died next? You got it; Uncle Mathew. Jollyamma apparently didn't appreciate people who questioned her word.

And, as far as motives go, there is also plain old convenience. In 2014, two-year-old Alphine Shaju died; Jollyamma, who was with her, initially said that the child had choked to death. Twenty months later, Alphine's mother, Sily, collapsed and died in Jollyamma's lap after drinking water Jolly had given to her while both were waiting outside a dentist's office. With these two out of the way, Joseph had a clear path to the object of her desire—the newly widowed husband and grieving father of Sily and Alphine. Less than a year later, the two married.

53. How Are Female Serial Killers *Like* Their Male Counterparts? Interestingly, a 2020 study found that prolific serial killers, both male and female, tend to exhibit an odd pattern of ebb and flow during their murderous careers. Comparing the murder timelines of 2,870 serial killers, researchers observed a steady pattern of escalation (the time between killing getting shorter) for victims one through four, pausing between victims four and five, escalating again for victims five through seven, and then pausing again between victims seven and eight. We don't really know why.

In terms of psychological similarities, we don't know a whole lot about the personalities of female serial killers. The little bit of research that has been done suggests that many of them have psychopathic personality traits, just like many male serial killers—charming, manipulative, cunning, deceitful, blaming others for their actions, exploitative, and lacking in empathy. As with men, many of them have a history of childhood trauma, most often abuse or neglect. And, like their male counterparts, female serial killers tend to choose vulnerable victims, i.e., victims who can't fight back.

The Sordid Saga of Patty Cannon

It's hard to find even a hint of a feminine wile in serial killer Patton Cannon. Born around 1760, in her early career she worked as a barmaid and a prostitute and, at some point, aspired to open a brothel. Legend has it, though, that her unpleasant personality did not endear her to her sex-seeking customers, forcing her to consider another career path. So, after the importation of slaves was outlawed in 1808, Cannon set her sights on illegal slave trading. Living on the Maryland/Delaware border was ideal; she was close enough to populations of freed or free African Americans and also not too far from slave-trading states.

From 1808 until her conviction for four murders (one of her husbands and three enslaved children) in 1829, Cannon and her associates tricked runaway slaves into thinking she was part of the Underground Railroad, kidnapped formerly freed slaves and sold them back into slavery, and snatched free black citizens and shipped them South to the slave trade. She and her gang are also believed to have murdered several wealthy visitors at the tavern she eventually owned. No one really knows how many deaths she was ultimately responsible for.

She was finally caught after a tenant on her farm discovered a chest full of human bones and an involuntary gang member, a slave who had been purchased by Cannon when he was seven and forced to lure unsuspecting victims into her trap, was caught and turned state's evidence. Scheduled to be hanged, she avoided the noose by three weeks, committing suicide via poison in her jail cell on May 11, 1829.

54. Has a Female Serial Killer Killed on a Man's Behalf? You already know that women have killed as part of a serial-killing team. This woman, though, became a team member after her serial killer boyfriend was already in jail. And her motive wasn't to help him kill; it was to "prove" his innocence. Her name was Veronica Lynn Compton and she moved from groupie to gruesome at lightning speed.

It all started in June 1980, when convicted serial killer Ken Bianchi received a letter from 23-year-old Veronica Lynn Compton, asking for his advice on a play she was writing about a female serial killer. Bianchi and his cousin, Angelo Buono, also known as the "Hillside Stranglers," were charged with the murder of twelve young women in Los Angeles and Bellingham, Washington in the late 1970s. Bianchi was in jail awaiting trial and the evidence against him was damning.

Compton and Bianchi continued to correspond and pen pal Compton fell madly in love. In fact, Compton became so enamored with Bianchi that she was willing to do anything to set her Romeo free. She hatched a plan to go back to Bellingham, Washington, strangling a random woman in the same way Bianchi had, and placing his semen inside the victim's vagina. That way, when investigators discovered this murder victim, and realized this murder perfectly matched Bianchi's other crime scenes, they would assume that the "real" killer was still on the loose and Bianchi was the wrong guy. In September 1980, Compton visited Bianchi, where she was given his semen in a rubber glove hidden in a book.

Using the alias "Karen," Compton found a victim: 26-year-old Kim Breed, whom she met in a Bellingham tavern. The two women hit it off and left the bar together. Compton accompanied Breed to the grocery store and then to Breed's house so she could feed her kids. Afterward, they continued drinking, snorting cocaine, and dancing with Breed's friends.

As the evening wore on, Compton eventually invited Breed for a drink in her hotel room, the Shangri-La, where Dr. Jekyll turned into Ms. Hyde and Compton attempted to strangle her new friend. She soon discovered, however, that strangling takes a lot of strength and, after a struggle, Breed escaped. Still trying to salvage the situation, Compton sent a letter to police proclaiming Bianchi's innocence and pointing to the botched murder attempt as evidence police had the wrong man (Bianchi). With Breed's help, though, police quickly connected the dots and arrested Compton for attempted first degree murder; she received a life sentence with the possibility of parole.

Compton was apparently a slow learner when it came to staying away from serial killers, however; during her prison term, she developed a romance with another sexual serial killer Doug Clark, who, along with his then-partner, Carol Bundy, killed at least six women in 1980. Although they got engaged, they did not marry and, in 1989, she married a history professor while she was still behind bars. Paroled in 1996, her parole was revoked after two weeks when she quit attending her mandated therapy, and, according to a social worker, painted pornographic murals on her three-year-old daughter's bedroom walls and answered the front door in the nude. She was paroled again in 2003.

Inspired by Serial Killers, Encouraged by Boyfriend

On May 11, 2020, twenty-eight-year old former Indiana corrections officer Kristen Wolf burst into an apartment at the Carriage House West Apartments complex in Indianapolis, Indiana and stabbed three people. Two of the three victims, a man and a woman in their twenties, died and a third was seriously in injured. Wolf did not know the victims but one of the victims had apparently dated Wolf's current boyfriend. (They later discovered he had also had a relationship with another woman in the same apartment complex).

A witness to the attacks told police Wolf had been wearing "wearing some kind of uniform with black tactical-style pants and a shirt with patches on it." She also wore a black knit hat which partially covered her face, allowing only her eyes to be seen. However, during the attack, Wolf's hat fell off, which had a patch with "Indiana Department of Corrections" and "Wolf" written on a tag; she was later identified, tracked down, and arrested.

When police searched Wolf's residence, they found numerous knives as well as some disturbing writings, including musings about what it would be like to kill someone, tales of drawing inspiration from serial killers, and a handwritten will. A former coworker stated that Wolf had gotten increasingly paranoid over the few weeks leading up to the attack and had, at one point, mentioned that her boyfriend "wasn't a good guy" because he was "always sending her (Wolf) messages about killing people."

Wolf's boyfriend, who was not named and not charged, had reportedly attempted to groom other women for murder. One of the surviving witnesses said that the deceased female victim had ended her relationship with him December 2019 because he became "too dark." According to court documents, this same man "was always talking about having a close group of friends who would kill each other" and had previously encouraged the female victim to slit her sister's throat. In January 2020, he had threatened the female victim, telling her "he had just got done with the girl he was training and that she was going to come over and cut them up."

One of the interesting things about this case is that the interactions between Wolf's boyfriend and his protégés seem to mimic how some team serial killers choose their accomplice. Based on witness accounts and if true, Wolf's boyfriend recruited at least three women into his killer training program. But, while a few of these women were willing to learn martial arts and listen to his dark rhetoric, the others drew the line at hurting anyone. It was only Wolf who was willing to act when push came to shove.

55. Who Do Female Serial Killers Kill? We've already talked about the fact that women tend to target people they know; they're pretty flexible when it comes to which friends or family members. They're equally likely to murder women and children as they are to kill men; in the U.S. more than half of female serial killers have had at least one female victim and more than 30 percent of them had murdered at least one child and a quarter had targeted the elderly and infirm.

It's also important to remember that, while female serial killers are much less likely to target strangers, some of them do; between 1800 and 2004, 31 percent of female serial killers killed at least one stranger—and sometimes for the oddest reasons. Southern California serial killer Dana Gray, (who murdered three women and attempted to murder one more in February and March 1994) for example, killed an acquaintance and two strangers to fund her shopping habit.

Cyanide Malika and Her Devout Victims

Forty-six-year-old K.D. Kempamma, who earned the nickname "Cyanide Malika" for the method she used to dispose of her victims, is serving a life term in India for killing seven women between 1999 and 2007 (five between October and December 2007, which is what led to her downfall). She started her criminal career as a thief, stealing from houses in which she worked as a maid. Her husband abandoned her in 1998, after she spent a year in jail for taking items from one of her employers.

No longer able to work as a housekeeper, she started a chit-fund company, an informal but legal system in India in which members all contribute money and, at the end of a certain period or when a contributor is in need of a loan, borrowers can bid on the money that has been collected. The fund is organized by the chit-fund organizer, who takes a fee. However, Kempamma's business failed, leaving her with huge debts and no way to make money.

This is when Kempamma really put her entrepreneurial ambitions to work, deciding to target women from rich families who were having personal problems, such as trouble getting pregnant or marital difficulties. Loitering around local temples, she would pose as a highly religious woman who had special influence with the gods. After she gained their trust, Kempamma would instruct these emotionally vulnerable women to meet her at a certain desolate location, wearing their finest clothes and most expensive jewelry to impress their deities, telling them she would make a special sacrifice for them. She would then perform these fake rituals, including serving them "holy water" which contained potassium cyanide, which was easily available as it is often used to clean gold. The women would die and Kempamma would steal their belongings.

It should be noted that death from cyanide is an extremely unpleasant way to die. First, your entire body starts to convulse. Then your mouth fills with a mixture of saliva, blood, and vomit. Then you pass out, and then you die. Your body is deprived of oxygen completely and you essentially suffocate to death. The entire process can take up to twenty minutes.

Kempamma was able to avoid arrest for as long as she did because she changed her name and identity each time she killed. However, she came to the attention of law enforcement after they received a tip expressing concern over Kempamma's tendency to hang around local temples and approach well-to-do worshippers; when they found and searched her, she still had jewelry from some of her victims. In 2012, Cyanide Mallika was convicted and sentenced to death.

56. Why Are Female Serial Killers Likely to Get Away with Murder Longer? You've probably spotted some clues to this question's answer already. Although a minority (20 percent) of female serial killers shoot their victims, for the most part, female serial killers kill *quietly*—they poison, they smother, they drown. Add this to fact that they tend to kill relatives, the elderly, or the ill, it's not surprising they are so hard to spot; whose mind would leap to murder when a three-month-old baby stops breathing or a middle-aged spouse drops dead of an apparent heart attack? Until the body count rises, these deaths are likely to be attributed to natural causes. And, of course, the icing on the cake is that female serial killers also benefit from stereotypes of women as kind and nurturing, making many people reluctant to suspect a woman even when suspicions of foul play are aroused.

57. What Female Serial Killer Has the Highest Victim Count? Recent history suggests that a serial killer's body count tends to be greater than what we initially think. Time and again, the crimes for which a suspected serial murderer is initially arrested turns out to be just the tip of the iceberg. However, when we go back in time, we often get the opposite effect; historical events become exaggerated.

Take Elizabeth Bathory, our previously discussed sixteenth-century Hungarian noblewoman, whose reputation as a short-tempered, cruel mistress is undoubtedly true, but whose current legacy as a sadist who bathed in virgins' blood in a vain attempt to preserve her youth, or as the current title holder in the Guinness Book of Records as the most murderous woman in history (she is given credit for six hundred murders), is likely based more on myth than fact. Our previously mentioned nineteenth century baby farmer, Amelia Dyer, is definitely a contender (having killed up to four hundred infants during her thirty-year career).

But if we're looking for accuracy, we're better off focusing on the past one hundred years. The few who stand out, in terms of sheer number of victims, have one thing in common; they murdered babies. For example, there's Japanese Miyuki Ishikawa, aka the Demon Midwife, who, along with several accomplices, killed over one hundred infants in the 1940s. Miyuki and her husband Takeshi extorted money from desperately poor parents who were faced with the task of raising an unwanted child; she assured them that the amount of money they paid her to get rid of the baby would be far less than the expense of raising it. A fake death certificate was included in the fee.

58. Are Female Serial Killers on the Decline? While the number of male serial killers is lower today than in the 1980s and 1990s, this is not necessarily true of female seral murderers. A 2015 analysis of sixty-four U.S. female serial killers between 1821 and 2008 found a 150 percent increase since 1975. However, let's not forget that, in 1900, 37.5 percent of all U.S. serial killers were women, three to five times the number we've had at any time over the last fifty years. Given the financial motives historically driving female serial killers, it's likely the women's liberation movement has not only freed some women, but also saved some men's lives.

PHOTOS

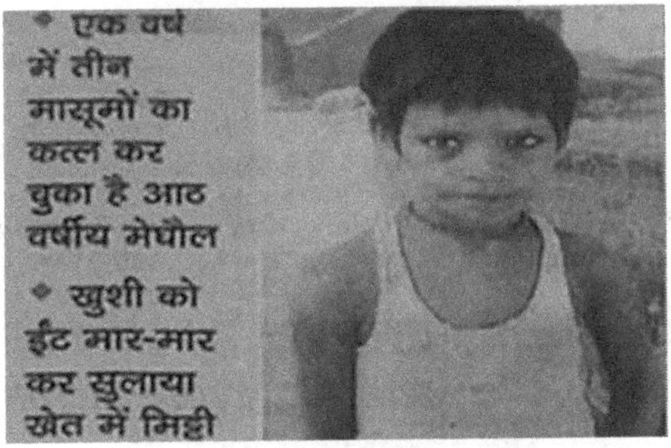

Indian serial killer, Amardeep Sada, believed to be the world's youngest serial killer. He killed his first victim at age 8.

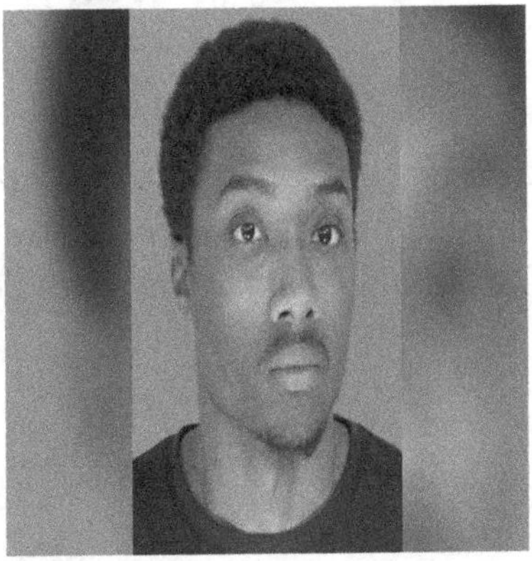

Khalil Wheever-Weaver, convicted of the murders of three women and the attempted murder pf a fourth, was tracked down by the family of his last victim, Sarah Butler.

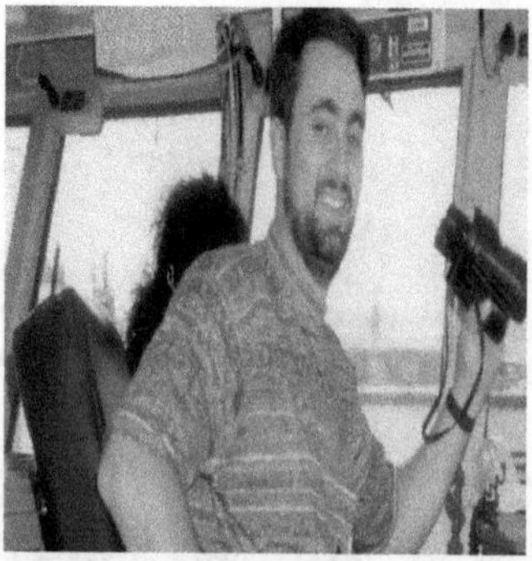

Australia was riveted by the trial of fifty-two-year old Bradley Robert Edwards, who was finally convicted in September 2020 of the rape and murders of two women in 1996 and 1996.

Described as a caring sister, cherished daughter and bright student, Jollyamma "Jolly" Joseph has been arrested for the murder of six family members between 2002 and 2016.

Canadian Dellen Millard is a testament to the fact that not all serial killers come from abusive background. Born and raised into a life of privilege and adoration, he was convicted of three murders, one of whom was his father.

Joseph James DeAngelo went from being a cop fired for shoplifting to a lifetime of increasingly violent crime as the Visalia Ransacker, East Area Rapist and Golden State Killer.

James Fairweather was just fifteen when he stabbed two strangers to death in a park. He was planning a third murder when he was caught.

In 2019, Michael Thomas Gargiulo, AKA the Hollywood Ripper, was convicted of the murders of two women and the attempted murder of a third. One of the witnesses against him was Ashton Kutcher, who was scheduled to go on a date with one of the victims the night she was murdered.

Con artists and financially-motivated serial killers, Ray (76) and Fay Copeland (69) were the oldest couple to receive the death penalty although both eventually died of natural causes.

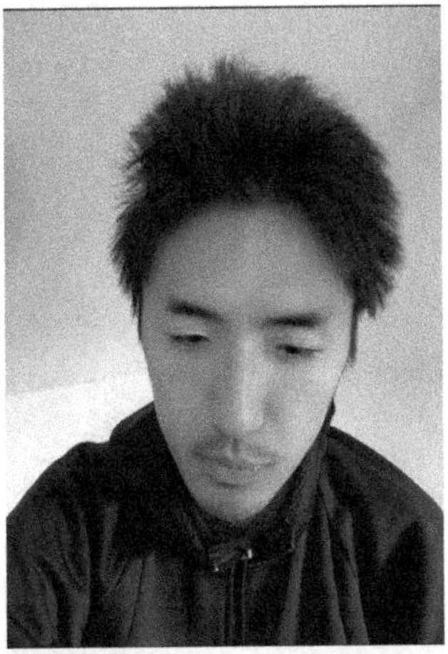

Japanese rapist and serial killer Takahiro Shiraishi found his victims on Twitter, targeting suicidal young women whom he lured to his home with a promise to help them die.

Stephane Bourgoin claimed to be a serial killer expert for years, claiming his wife's murder was a motivator for his expertise and he had spent years researching serial murder and interviewing serial killers. In 2020, almost all of his claims were debunked.

Samuel Little is currently believed to be the most prolific serial killer in the United States. He has confessed to ninety-three murders between 1970 and 2005; at least fifty have been confirmed.

In 2016, registered nurse and Canada's only known healthcare serial killer Elizabeth Wettlaufer confessed to killing eight patients by injecting her victims with insulin.

After Alaskan serial killer Israel Keyes killed himself in 2012 while in custody and awaiting trial, prison officials found drawings of eleven skulls in Keyes' own blood in his cell.

Diane Staudte, with the help of her favorite daughter Rachel, systematically poisoned to death husband Mark and attempted to poison daughter Sarah.

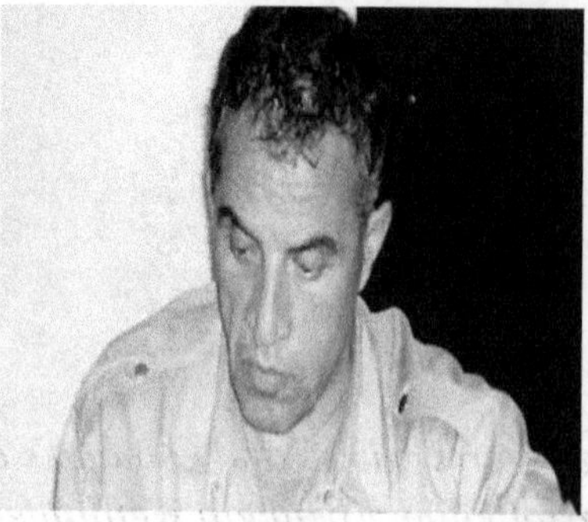

Macedonian serial killer Vlado Taneski's career as a journalist as he covered the murders he was actually committing.

Juana Barazza was a Mexican former professional wrestler and serial killer dubbed La Mataviejitas ("The Old Lady Killer") who was sentenced to 759 years in prison for killing between 42 and 48 elderly women.

Javed Iqbal was a Pakistani serial killer who confessed to the sexual abuse and murder of 100 boys, ranging in age from 6 to 16.

Heriberto "Eddie" Seda is an American serial killer who struck New York City from 1990 to 1993. Although he claimed to be the Zodiac killer, it quickly became apparent that he was a copycat. Before being caught on June 18, 1996, Seda killed three people and wounded five others.

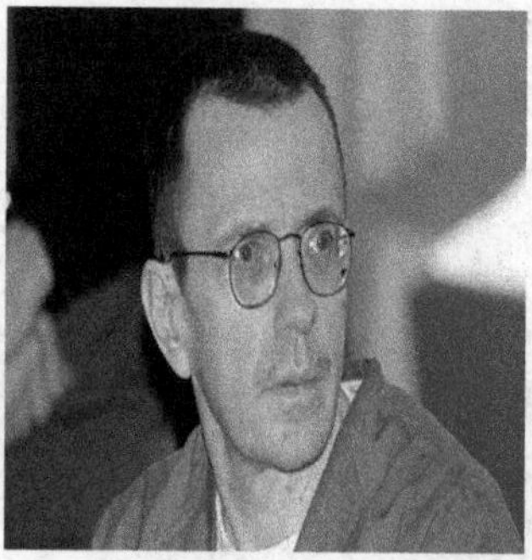

John Paul Franklin channeled his racist ideology into serial killing hate crimes.

Part 4: Serial Killers from Around the World.

More than half of serial killers (that we know about) come from English-speaking countries. Aside from the U.S., these countries round out the top ten in terms of having the most serial killers: England, South Africa, Canada, Italy, Japan, Germany, Australia, Russia, and India.

59. What Should We Do with Teenage Serial Killers?

Meet James Fairweather, England's youngest serial killer. He was just fifteen when, in March of 2014, he stabbed a father of five, James Attfield, one hundred and two times. Mr. Attfield was a vulnerable victim; he was still recovering from a serious head injury he had received in a horrific car accident four years earlier and he had fallen asleep at a nearby park after having several drinks at a pub. Three months later, Fairweather murdered Nahid Almanea, a 31-year-old female Saudi Arabian student, with a bayonet. Almanea was walking along a nature trail in broad daylight when she was attacked and murdered.

Fairweather didn't know either one of his victims; they were complete strangers. He was finally arrested a year later loitering in the bushes at a local park, apparently looking for another victim. A concerned dog owner thought something was odd and called the police, who discovered Mr. Fairweather wearing gloves and carrying a knife.

Fairweather was clearly a troubled teen. People who knew him described him as a relatively normal child but said that, as he approached adolescence, he was often bullied because of his physical appearance (his ears slightly protruded) and his awkward social skills. (During his trial, at least one forensic mental health professional who evaluated him believes he may have had an undiagnosed autism spectrum disorder.) By age thirteen, Fairweather was a loner, spending hours playing video games and watching horror movies. By fourteen, he had become obsessed with violent porn and serial killers.

Classmates during his most recent school year described an increasingly scary peer who threatened to carry out a Columbine-style gun massacre and once told classmates he wanted to be a "murderer" when he grew up. Three months before his first murder, he had been convicted of armed (with a knife) robbery of a convenience store; he was sentenced to twelve months of youth supervision three days before his first murder.

What they did not see, though, was someone who seemed "crazy." Before his murders, no one saw any evidence Fairweather was hearing voices or suffering from delusions, symptoms he later claimed drove him to commit murders. Trust me; people who are actively psychotic tend to stand out. They respond out loud to the voices they hear; they tell others about the strange beliefs or thoughts that are upsetting or influencing them. Their symptoms often impact their behavior in other ways; if they believe someone is following them, for example, they may alter their normal route, get a security camera, or alert police. Not a single person who knew Fairweather before his murders thought he had lost touch with reality.

In spite of this, three defense psychiatrists testified at trial that they believed James was suffering from a psychotic illness. The prosecutor's expert was having none of it; he testified that Fairweather's descriptions of his psychotic symptoms sounded like something out of a horror movie and said that, in his opinion, Fairweather's actions before, during, and after the crime were premeditated, intentional, and deliberate. The jury wholeheartedly agreed and Fairweather was convicted. In 2016, the judge, citing his belief that Fairweather's true diagnosis was a budding psychopathic personality disorder, sentenced him to two life sentences with a mandatory 27-year minimum.

But back to the larger question about what we should do with future Fairweathers. First of all, most juvenile murderers are serial-killer wannabes. We should always be cautious about labeling youthful offenders as psychopaths. The teen years are a time of personal and emotional change and, in comparison to adults, adolescent psychopathy scores are less stable. As teens mature, their scores on psychopathy tests often decrease. Better to avoid labeling someone with a pretty grim diagnosis than run the risk of stigmatizing someone who is going through a tumultuous time as a teenager that she or he will grow out of.

On the other hand, psychopathy doesn't just pop up out of nowhere once a person reaches voting age. Some research suggests that callous-unemotional personality traits can be spotted by age five and are relatively stable throughout adolescence and adulthood. In fact, if we ignore the delinquent behaviors that are common to both to psychopathy and a troubled teen and just count the personality traits (lack of empathy and remorse, irresponsibility, impulsivity, manipulative interpersonal style) that are associated with psychopathy, some of them are pretty obvious, even during the tumultuous teen years.

60. How Often Do Serial Killers Use Drugs to Control a Victim? ***(England)*** We've all heard horror stories of a young girl out at a party or bar, someone slips something in her drink, and she is sexually assaulted by one (or more) of the perpetrators. Before she left for college, my daughter heard more than her share of warnings and admonishments and left home armed with a liquid product that can sniff out a date-rape drug in a drink with one single drop.

So, it probably isn't surprising that some serial killers have also drugged their victims as a way to gain control over them. Stephen Port's modus operandi was to trawl gay-dating apps such as Grindr, arrange to have sex, and then knock his targets out with secretly administered doses of gamma hydroxybutyrate (GHB) in their alcoholic drinks. In 2016, the London-based Port was sentenced to life in prison for the murders of four men and the sexual assault of several others in 2014 and 2015. He was eventually arrested when a closed-circuit camera caught him and his last victim walking together near a railway station shortly before the victim died. All of the victims had massive amounts of drugs in their system.

Here's an example once again of where truth is stranger than fiction. Port himself had once been a victim of a man named Gerald Matovu, who had slipped Port the same date rape drug (GHB) and robbed him. In spite of this, at some point their relationship shifted from perpetrator-victim to drug dealer-client and Matovu was arrested, and convicted, for illegally selling GHB to Port. After Matovu had served his time, he proceeded to drug and rob his way across London, ultimately killing fifty-four-year-old father of three, Eric Michels, during one of his attacks. Ironically, Gerald Matovu was the first person since Port to be convicted of murder with a fatal overdose of the drug GHB.

61. Why Do Serial Killers Use Religion as a Reason to Kill? ***(South Africa)*** Both the kindest and the cruelest acts known to man have been done in the name of religion. Sometimes religion is used to get someone to drop his or her guard (see Cyanide Malika from India), sometimes it's a religious leader doing the evil deed (think Charles Manson), and sometimes—rarely—a person commits a crime while under the influence of religious delusions (see my earlier tale of Henry Mullins) Sometimes, though, religion is just an excuse for why an evil deed was done (such as a human sacrifice).

The Zulu people of South Africa believe in the existence of Tokoloshe, tiny, evil-spirited, hairy, half-animal/half-humans. They are believed to be so powerful that, should you encounter one and look in his eyes, you would immediately drop dead. Should a Tokoloshe ask you to something, you cannot refuse to grant him his wishes. So, if someone commits robbery, rape, or murder, and can convince the community that a Tokoloshe made him do it, the offense may be overlooked.

Apparently, this was Elifasi Msomi's strategy. Elifasi Msomi was a weak sangoma (medicine man) looking to be more powerful. While seeking the guidance of another shaman, he claimed to have been possessed by a Tokoloshe. In this state of possession, Msomi allegedly went on an 18-month killing spree between 1953 and 1955. His first crime was raping and killing a young girl in the presence of his mistress. As she called the police, he managed to escape.

After mutilating and murdering five children, he was caught but managed to escape again. He managed to stay on the loose for a month before being captured. In his trial, he claimed to be a pawn for the Tokoloshe's evil deeds. However, since body parts are necessary for most sangoma treatments, it was suspected that he was killing children to sell their body parts. Two psychologists also claimed that Elifasi knew what he was doing and got sexual gratification from inflicting pain. He was convicted of five murders and sentenced to die by hanging. Several local Zulu chiefs asked to be present during the hanging to make sure that the evil spirit had departed.

Msomi hasn't been the only serial killer to use religion to justify their murders; on August 11, 2020, nineteen-year-old Nigerian, Sunday Shodipe, was arrested for murdering five women. He claims he did it under the orders of an "herbalist," who told him he needed sacrifices to appease spirits who were tormenting him and "sucking his blood."

So far, the herbalist, Baba Akinyele, has denied this (but has also been arrested).

But what is more common than using religion to *justify* murder is the use of religion to *lure* their victims to it. South African serial killer Jack Mogale (2008-2009), aka "the West End Serial Killer," seduced his sixteen victims by claiming that he was a Zion Christian prophet and preacher. He would offer them a ride, preaching to them and helping them to feel safe. Once they reached their destination, however, his religious persona would evaporate and he would rape and then either beat or strangle them to death.

The Strange Case of Americans Lori Vallow and Charles Daybell

It's not hard to spot strange beliefs if you're looking across cultures. But when they're close to home, they can be hard to swallow. Take the Vallow/ Daybell case. From all appearances, Lori Vallow was a devout Mormon, loving wife, and devoted mother until she met Chad Daybell in the fall of 2018. Chad, also Mormon, had written a number of doomsday books beginning in 2014 that were intended for a traditional Church of Jesus Christ of Latter-Day Saints audience.

Between 2014 and 2018, two things happen; Chad begins to attract followers from the LDS community and his teachings begin to drift from typical Mormon beliefs. He talks of two near-death experiences that have allegedly "opened the veil" between this world and the next, he asserts that he receives direct messages from God, and he predicts the end times will occur in July 2020, during which he will lead 144,0000 believers to meet the second coming of Christ. Lori is apparently captivated by Chad's teachings and, when she meets him in person in late 2018, by the man himself.

In early 2019, Lori's behavior became increasingly bizarre, so much so that Lori's then-husband, Charles Vallow, petitions the court to have her involuntarily evaluated by a mental health professional to see if she is having a mental breakdown. She is evaluated and released. The two eventually separate in the spring of 2019, and things go from bad to worse.

Five months later, husband Charles is dead, shot by Lori's brother, Alex, allegedly in self-defense. Lori's seven-year-old son, JJ, and 16-year-old daughter, Tylee, disappear in September 2019. Tammy Daybell, Chad's former wife, dies suddenly and mysteriously in October 2019; Chad and Lori wed a few weeks later. The two children are found buried in Chad Daybell's backyard in June 2020.

Around all of these murders have swirled allegations of a doomsday cult, spiritual prophecies, and beliefs in zombies and teleportation. Writings have emerged in which Chad evaluated Lori's friends and family members according to how "light" or "dark" they were. Chad and Lori are currently awaiting trial for conspiracy to conceal, destroy, or alter evidence in connection with the deaths of the two children; both have pleaded not guilty. The investigations into all of the deaths are ongoing; murder charges are likely.

62. Has There Ever Been an Immigrant Serial Killer? ***(South Africa, U.S.A.)*** Possibly, and if so, it happened right here in the U.S. Brian Steven Smith, a South African native and American resident, has not been convicted of a crime, although in October 2019 he was indicted for the murder of two native Alaskan women: thirty-year-old Kathleen Henry and fifty-two-year old Veronica Abouchuk. At this point, I don't think either country wants to claim him, but he did become a naturalized U.S. citizen in September 2019.

The murders were first brought to the attention of both police and the wider public when an SD card labeled *Homicide at Midtown Marriott* was found on a street in Anchorage, Alaska. (An SD or Security Digital card is a way of transferring and storing data on a phone, camera, or portable tablet). The card was extremely disturbing, containing violent, graphic images and videos of a woman being raped, beaten, and murdered. It was immediately handed over to police for further investigation.

As you might imagine, there are not a lot of South African expatriates living in Alaska. As a result, Smith's unusual accent in the video stood out, and police narrowed their suspect pool. Police quickly linked Smith to a rented hotel room with carpet that matched that seen in the video and an older-model Ford Ranger pickup truck, also visible in the recovered video. The alleged serial killer, who is in jail and awaiting trial, faces a possible ninety-nine years in prison if found guilty of the charges leveled against him, including first- and second-degree murder, sexual assault, tampering with physical evidence and "misconduct involving a corpse."

The "Kebab" Serial Murders

Between 2000 and 2007, seven Turkish immigrants and one Greek were murdered in seven different cities across Germany. The only connection between them seemed to be their ethnic background and the fact that many of them owned or worked in small businesses—a tailor, a kebab restaurant, a grocery store, a flower shop, an internet cafe. All were shot several times in the face at close range with the same gun; no one knew why.

German police dubbed these murders the "kebab" murders and quickly concluded that they were hits from the Turkish mafia over turf wars, in spite of the fact that none of the victims had a criminal history and there was no evidence of Mafia involvement. They also dismissed eyewitness reports of two European men leaving the scenes of the crimes. In 2011, the killer or killers, apparently frustrated by the fact that the clues they had left behind for police had been ignored, sent several German newspapers a video with images of the 1960s *Pink Panther* cartoon interspersed with news footage of the actual crime scenes and photos of the victims. The end of the video concluded with the outright suggestion that a far-right group, the National Socialist Underground (NSU)—not the Turkish Mafia—was responsible. Essentially, the killers, wanting credit, confessed.

On November 4, 2011, a bank-robbery-gone-wrong resulted in the recovery of the gun used in the previously unsolved murders. An investigation linked the right-wing extremists to Nazi paraphernalia, weapons manuals, and a backlash against foreigners. Two of the "kebab killers" committed suicide before they could be arrested but, in 2019, the remaining assassin, Beate Zschape, was sentenced to life in prison. The immigrant community was outraged that the police had immediately made assumptions about the victims instead of following the evidence, proclaiming that racism had been as much a part of the investigation as it was a motive for the murders themselves.

63. Are Some Serial Killers Products of Overindulgent Families? ***(Canada)*** Most serial killers have childhoods filled with deprivation, poverty, and trauma, which ultimately warps their adulthood. Not so with Dellen Millard. He started out with every advantage. He was an only child whose parents doted on him. He went to private schools, took swanky vacations, and dabbled with expensive hobbies. In fact, Millard's mother, Madeline Burns, once compared his birth to Mufasa holding up Simba—the new lion king—for the world to admire. When it comes to parental attention, perhaps there *is* too much of a good thing.

As Millard grew older, nothing satisfied him. He sought out one thrill after another, from off-road racing to skydiving to jumping off of roofs at pool parties. After dabbling in a number of legitimate jobs, he found his real passion—theft. The young man with money to burn took delight in planning and executing heists, using his charm and financial resources along the way to collect a group of malleable followers along with his stolen goods. When theft lost its luster, he moved on to murder.

So how could someone with such promise wind up in prison? Millard's life wasn't completely charmed. His parents divorced when he was eleven. There appeared to be a deep rift between his father and his uncle that never healed. But he may have had too much of some things. While no child can get too much love, he/she can get too much praise and special treatment. In fact, research suggests that parents who overvalue their children tend to raise youngsters with an overblown sense of their own superiority. They become narcissistic because their parents put them on a pedestal and—because they are repeatedly told they are special or deserve better treatment than others—they come to believe they should be on that pedestal forever.

Just as childhood poverty and abuse can stamp out a child's innate empathy, there are certain parenting traps that can cultivate a child's worst qualities. These traps, and the maladaptive messages that accompany them, are seductive; they come disguised as love and kindness. But the damage they can do is ugly:

> **a. There's no one as special as you.** Parents who communicate consistent appreciation for the unique person their child is tend to raise a child who feels secure in his or her own worth and who appreciates the worth of other people in his or her life. On the other hand, nothing good comes out of teaching a child he or she is more special than others.
>
> Parents who overvalue their children tend to exaggerate their child's qualities and indiscriminately lavish their child with praise. Millard's mother's letter in support of her son, even after three first-degree-murder convictions, suggests a parent whose description of her son is more of a fantasy than a reality. Without a doubt, she is in an extremely difficult and distressing position; no mother wants to think her child is capable of such atrocities. But it is possible to love your child and still face the truth.
>
> In her letter submitted to the court, Madeline Burns described her son as a "gentle spirit" who was a boy genius and "empathically served the needs of others." This is not how others saw him. Early school friends described him as somewhat awkward and attention-seeking, a tall, husky kid who had some trouble speaking and pronouncing

certain words. During the trial, Millard's maternal uncle described him as a "sick, twisted prick."

b. The rules don't apply to you. Well-meaning parents can confuse love with leniency, failing to set clear expectations about what is expected of them and protecting a child from much-needed consequences for unacceptable behavior. Taken to the extreme, they indulge and/or enable their child when he or she is being selfish, insensitive, and/or uncaring. Not only does this deprive a child of the opportunity to learn from their mistakes, but it can lead a child to grow up without a sense of right or wrong or a sense of remorse when causing someone harm.

There's a lot we don't know about Millard's childhood. We don't know what kind of boundaries his parents tried to set or what kind of friendships they encouraged. We do know that, as an adult, he collected followers rather than friends. We do know the people he surrounded himself with were those he could control through charm or money and in which loyalty was the highest value. The lengths Millard's groupies were willing to go to just to get him his thrills was pretty amazing.

Even the most well-adjusted child behaves badly at times. No one wins when parents deny their child's capacity for misbehavior and disallow consequence—they send the message that the child need not ever consider the effects of their behavior on others. Dellen Millard seemed to have no qualms about killing. And yet, in spite of three murder convictions and an overwhelming body of evidence, his mother continues to believe her son is being framed.

64. How Often Do Sexually Motivated Serial Killers Target Gay Men? ***(Canada)*** Most sexually motivated serial killers are heterosexual and most of the victims are women (sixty-five percent). It's hard to get percentages on the number of strictly gay serial killers because there are all kinds of confounding variables; whether or not the killer is "out," for example. Of the serial killers who targeted men, forty-two percent were homosexual and the rest were a mixture of female serial killers, revenge seekers, thrill murderers, and health care killers.

But there have been serial killers who specifically targeted *gay* men. Jeffrey Dahmer was probably the most infamous serial killer to target gay men; he always insisted he killed his seventeen victims (1978-91) because he didn't want them to leave. Others have targeted gay men for a myriad of reasons: to be famous (Collin Ireland, who murdered five gay men in England in 1993), for sexual gratification (Stephen Port, John Wayne Gacy), and even for revenge (Gary Ray Bowles; murdered six gay men in 1994).

One of the most recent was Canadian Bruce McArthur, who, in February 2019, pleaded guilty to the murder of eight men in Toronto. All of the men McArthur killed between 2010 and 2017 were sexually assaulted first. Many were immigrants from South Asia or the Middle East who were not "out" to their families and would secretly visit Toronto's gay village for support and companionship. Instead, they were murdered.

Members of the gay community were outraged that McArthur was active for seven years. Many think McArthur's killing career began long before 2010; it is virtually unheard of for a serial killer to start killing at age fifty-six and the carefully-planned way he carried out his crimes suggested this was not his first rodeo. Many also believed that police didn't care about the victims because they were gay and, as a result, didn't fully investigate. There seems to be some evidence to support this.

A judicial order unsealed in February 2019 showed that Toronto police knew McArthur "had a link" to three of the eight men he eventually murdered as early as 2013 but had shut down their investigation in April 2014 when investigators failed to find any incriminating evidence connecting McArthur to the missing men. While we might chalk that up to bad luck, it was a lot harder for police officers to explain why they released McArthur in 2016 after a man called 911 saying McArthur had tried to strangle him during consensual sex. When questioned by police, McArthur brushed it off as a miscommunication about sexual preferences and the matter was dropped. At least one Toronto police officer was later charged with neglect of duty and insubordination over the poorly handled 2016 investigation.

65. What Is One of the Strangest Motives You've Ever Heard for Serial Murder? ***(Italy)*** Italian serial killer Leonarda Cianciulli committed horrific acts with the bodies of the three women she killed in 1939 and 1940. When they were discovered, people who knew her were stunned. For all appearances, Cianciulli was a sweet little lady who served her friends and neighbors homemade tea cakes and was a devoted mother to her four children. Hiding behind that caring veneer, however, was a fraudulent, superstitious schemer who believed in the magical properties of human sacrifice and who was not averse to breaking the law to make a profit. Born on April 18, 1894, Cianciulli's life seemed doomed from the start. Her mother, Emilia, was raped and became pregnant; rather than endure the shame of single motherhood, she was forced to marry her rapist, Cianciulli's father. Tragically and somewhat understandably, Cianciulli's mother never bonded with her daughter. Even after Cianciulli's father died and Emilia remarried, she was cold and emotionally abusive toward her. By the time Cianciulli reached adulthood, she had attempted suicide twice.

Things might have turned around for Cianciulli had she chosen to marry one of the financially secure men her mother and stepfather picked out for her. Instead, Cianciulli fell in love with a penniless man (Raffaele Pansardi) her parents disapproved of, married him, and moved away. Throughout the rest of her life, Cianciulli believed that all of her misfortunes were a result of her mother's cursing her for choosing the wrong man.

And plenty of misfortunes there were. In 1927, Cianciulli was jailed for fraud. She and her husband lost one house to an earthquake. Pregnant seventeen times, she suffered three miscarriages and lost ten of her children before they were teenagers. After sixteen years of marriage, her husband deserted her and her four remaining children.

By this time, though, things were not all bad. Cianciulli was living in the small town of Correggio, where she was popular with her neighbors. She had a small but thriving soap shop and moonlighted as a fortune teller and hypnotist. She also visited palm readers and psychics herself, just to make sure she and her remaining children were safe, especially her beloved favorite son, Giuseppe.

According to a long memoir Cianciulli penned in prison, her murderous career began after a fellow fortune teller told Cianciulli that she needed to make human sacrifices or all of her remaining children would die (this *was* in the middle of World War II). To allegedly keep her kids from perishing, she lured three separate middle-aged women, each who had frequently sought her psychic advice, to her house through false promises of a job or a suitor. Before she offed them, she would have them secretly prepare to move to a new town (where the exciting opportunity awaited) and instruct them to write letters to friends and family in advance of their relocation, which she generously offered to mail. She would then have them come by her house for a final visit, give them a drugged glass of wine, and kill them with an axe. The most infamous part of her story was the process by which she used part of the blood and fat, along with caustic soda, to make flour for her infamous tea cakes.

I should mention that there are some people who do not believe Cianciulli's altruistic explanation and think her real motive for murder was financial (she robbed each of her victims and their houses afterward) and not spiritual. And that the dramatic confessions in her book were just an attempt to make her look more desperate and sympathetic at her trial. Whatever the true motive, she was finally arrested after her last victim's sister-in-law became suspicious and told authorities that Cianciulli was the last person the victim had been seen with. She died in a criminal insane asylum on October 15, 1970 at age seventy-six, having served thirty years in prison and three years in a forensic psychiatric hospital.

Serial-Killer Journalist Reports on His Own Murders

A story about a serial killer who murders so he can write about it sounds like a bad novel. But that pretty much sums up at least part of the motive driving Vlado Taneski, award-winning journalist for a Macedonia newspaper and murderer of at least three elderly women between 2005 and 2008; given the brutal way in which his victims were tortured and raped, sexual sadism was likely another.

Taneski's writing career got a huge boost when he began covering the murders. He pitched the story to his editors, showed up at crime scenes, and interviewed surviving family members. In his articles, he pondered possible abduction scenarios. He was even one of the first journalists to suggest the murders were linked. He covered the trial of two men arrested for the murder of one of the victims, pointing out that they had been in jail when the murder occurred and, as such, could not be guilty.

Unfortunately for Taneski, he apparently lost track of what the police had revealed versus what he, as the murderer, knew. It was this inside knowledge which led to his downfall. Over the three years Taneski covered the crimes, police gradually noticed that Taneski's articles contained information—the type of cord used to strangle the women, the order in which the victims were murdered, and so forth—that they had deliberately withheld from the public.

A search warrant found incriminating evidence and his DNA matched semen found at the crime scenes. On June 23, 2008, just one day after his arrest, Taneski was found dead inside his cell, a suicide note tucked under his pillow.

66. Have Any Serial Killers Worshiped the Devil? "The devil made me do it." How many times have horrific acts, including murder and child abuse, had Satan's name attached to them? A lot.

Not all of them *really* involved the devil. In some of the most famous cases of alleged Satanic worship, the label seems to have been either thrown around by a media horrified at the cruelty or gore attached to a serial killer's actions, or the killer himself threw devil worship into the mix for shock value or to justify clearly self-interested acts. In 1995, for example, 18-year-old Christa Pikes, who had apparently toyed with the occult, blamed the devil for her decision to take out a love rival. In reality, jealousy seemed to be a more likely motive. All had been well until Pike's 19-year-old fellow Job Corps (a program for troubled teens) student, Colleen Slemmer, began talking a little too much to Pike's boyfriend. In January 1995, Pike and two others, including seventeen-year old boyfriend, Tadaryl Shipp and a female friend, promised Slemmer pot and a video and killed her with a box cutter, cleaver, and slab of asphalt.

Convicted and sentenced to death in 1996, Pike had hardly been an ideal prisoner; in 2001, she was given an additional twenty-five years for the attempted murder of another inmate. But there has been no mention of devil worship since Pike has been incarcerated. Worshiping Satan, in this case, seemed to be just another way to rebel against authority and express anger over her well-documented history of abuse and neglect.

Even Richard Ramirez, the original Night Stalker, who, in the media, was the poster child for the dark angel, seemed to be more influenced by his cousin Mike than Lucifer. Mike, a Vietnam vet, filled his young protégé's head with violence. Among his favorite images were photographs of young Vietnamese women forced to give Mike "blow jobs," followed by pictures of the same women, now decapitated. Topping this off was thirteen -year old Ramirez's witnessing Mike shoot his wife to death.

But there *have* been serial killers who seemed sincere in their Satanic beliefs and whose crimes were believed to be a part of their "spiritual practices." For example, between 1998 and 2004, two members of the aptly named Italian rock band Beasts of Satan, Andrea Volpe and Pietro Guerrieri, committed a series of Satanic murders.

On January 17, 1998, 19-year-old Chiara Marino was stabbed to death under a full moon in a wooded area near Milan; investigators believe she may have been chosen because she resembled depictions of the Virgin Mary. Her boyfriend was beaten to death with a hammer when he tried to save her. On January 24, 2004, 27-year-old Mariangela Pezzotta, an ex-girlfriend of Andrea Volpe, was shot and buried alive. Apparently even those who rely on dark supernatural powers have worldly concerns; the motive for Pezzotta's murder appears to have been concerns that she knew too much about the group's activities, particularly the previous murders, and couldn't be trusted to keep her mouth shut.

Was Serial Killer Pazuzu Algarad a Real Satanist?

Before Algarad was a serial-killing, self-proclaimed devil worshipper, he was mentally ill Jason Lawson, a troubled child and adolescent born on August 12, 1978. From all accounts, Lawson exhibited early behavior problems and began using drugs and alcohol at age thirteen. At various points growing up, he had received a number of psychiatric diagnoses, including agoraphobia, bipolar disorder, and schizophrenia. But he never got consistent mental health treatment, which his mother has claimed was due to the family's limited financial resources.

After dropping out of school in the ninth grade, his mental health continued to deteriorate. By 2002, twenty-four-year old Lawson had changed his name in honor of the demon Pazuzu who tormented Regan MacNeil in the movie *The Exorcist* and became a full-fledged devil worshipper at his North Carolina home. His appearance and behavior became increasingly bizarre; he filed his teeth into points and got facial tattoos. He sacrificed animals, performed rituals during full moons, and, gradually, collected a small group of followers to participate in his orgies and blood-drinking. Sometime after June 1, 2009, he killed a man who was staying at his house and, the same year, he participated in the murder of a second one. Both were drifters who had hung around Pazuzu's place to party and use drugs.

Algarad constantly bragged that he had committed a number of criminal activities: rape, murder, assault. Some of his followers didn't believe him, apparently due to his reputation for doing and saying things for their shock value and also because he was a chronic liar. Some did; one of his friends eventually contacted police to report that Algarad had said there were bodies buried in his backyard. On October 4, 2014, the decomposed bodies of his two victims were discovered. Pazuzu, charged with two counts of first-degree murder, committed suicide in his jail cell on October 28, 2015, allegedly on a full moon.

But was he really a Satanist? After Algarad's arrest (and the resulting media frenzy), many practicing Satanists not only condemned Algarad's actions but also the media's tendency to link Algarad's actions with their religion. In addition, there was no evidence that Algarad was a member of a Satanic Temple or had studied genuine Satanic practices. So, was Algarad really a Satanist or was this an expression of his mental illness? Not even his followers seem to know.

67. If a Serial Killer Targeted Only People Who Wanted to Die, Is That Murder? (*Japan*) Research consistently shows that most suicidal people don't really want to die; they just want their pain to stop. If they can get help or stave off their self-destructive thoughts long enough, things get better and life improves. In fact, nine out of ten people who attempt suicide will not die by it and seventy percent will never try it again. Suicide prevention was of no concern to 29-year-old Takahirio Shiraishi, though. Although he pretended to care about the emotional well-being of the suicidal victims he found on social media, what he really wanted to do was to rape, rob, and murder them.

Shiraishi would first find a depressed young woman on Twitter. He would respond sympathetically to one of her public comments about suicide. He would then encourage her to go off of Twitter and communicate directly with him, arguing this would allow the two of them to have a more personal and detailed conversation. His real goal was to get his victim to become psychologically dependent on him. He was good at it; once the one-on-one communication started, he would pretend to disclose personal information about himself, including his own "depression" and "suicidal thoughts." He would offer to help his "friend" commit suicide if she was really serious about it, while at the same time reassuring her that he would never rush her. Heck, he would propose, they could even end their lives at the same time!

Shiraishi was extremely persuasive. In fact, Yasushi Sugihara, a professor of clinical psychology at Kyoto University who analyzed some two hundred messages exchanged via a social networking service between Shiraishi and one of his suicidal victims found that Shiraishi used techniques typically employed by counselors to gain the trust of suicidal victims—establishing rapport, asking questions to understand his victim's vulnerabilities, and so forth.

After he had his victim hooked, Shiraishi would invite her over to his apartment, where he would sexually assault her, strangle her, and steal her money. He killed and dismembered eight women and one man, ranging in age from fifteen to twenty-six, between August and October 2017. He was caught after police, who were investigating one of the missing women, discovered she had been seen walking with Shiraishi shortly before she vanished. His victims' bodies were discovered inside containers in his apartment. Luckily, his last target survived because she declined his offer for the two of them to meet in person.

68. Should a Serial Killer Be Put to Death if They No Longer Remember the Crimes? ***(Japan)*** From 1994 to 2013, Chisako Kakehi murdered all the men she dated, at least eight (although she was only convicted for killing three). She was even married to some of them. She was finally arrested in 2014 after her dead fourth husband's body was found loaded with cyanide. Kakehi loudly proclaimed her innocence but the police found a bag of cyanide in a plant pot she ditched near her home. The trail of dead bodies behind her and the discovery that she had received $7 million in insurance payouts didn't help her, either.

Kakehi, of course, pleaded not guilty. But then, out of the blue during her 2017 trial, she confessed on the witness stand, telling her stunned audience that she had no intention of hiding what she had done and declaring that she killed her husband out of pure hatred. Her attorneys were horrified.

Two days later, she walked it all back, saying she had no memory of what she had said and would have no idea of how to kill anyone. Her defense attorneys, clearly in a quandary, told the judge that Kakehi had dementia and, as such, should not be convicted. No one bought this argument and she was sentenced to death.

But what if she really did have it? If this had happened in the United States and Kakehi *did* have dementia, the outcome might have been different. On February 27, 2019, the Supreme Court ruled that the Eighth Amendment of our

Constitution forbids the execution of a prisoner who does not have "a rational understanding of the reason for [his] execution," irrespective of its cause. The ruling reversed a decision of the Alabama state courts that would have permitted the execution of Vernon Madison, a death-row prisoner whose multiple strokes in 2015 and 2016 resulted in vascular dementia and left him with no memory of the crime for which he was sentenced to death—and no ability to understand why he is on death row.

The Transgender Murder Defense: I'm Not the Same Person I Was When I Killed

Most transgender men and women who are involved in murder are victims. In fact, according to the American Medical Association, transgender hate crimes, including homicide, are on the rise. In 2019, at least twenty-six transgender or gender-non-conforming people were fatally shot or killed by other violent means. During the first seven months of 2020, the total number of murdered transgendered women has already surpassed the previous year. Dallas police even wondered if there was a serial killer targeting black transgender women after three were found dead between October 2018 and May 2019; it now appears they were unrelated murders.

It's important to keep this backdrop in mind when we talk about Donna Perry. In July, 2017, 65-year-old Donna R. Perry was sentenced to life without the possibility of parole for the 1990 murders of three sex workers in Spokane, Washington. But, back then, there *was* no Donna.

These murders were unsolved for more than two decades; finally, in 2012, Perry was linked through DNA to all three victims. At the time of her arrest, Perry denied having anything to do with their deaths. However, investigators uncovered a cellmate who, in 1998, served time with Perry in an Oregon prison. According to an affidavit provided by the ex-cellmate, Perry told him at the time that he was a "sociopath" and confessed to killing nine prostitutes because "she couldn't breed but those women had the ability to have children and they were wasting it being 'pond scum.'"

But in 1990, Donna was *Douglas* Perry. When faced with the overwhelming evidence against her, Perry stated that she was not the same person who killed back in 1990 and that she had intentionally sought out gender-reassignment surgery in 2000 "as a permanent way to control violence." Transgender advocates were furious, calling Perry's statements a desperate defense ploy and accurately pointing out that there is no link between gender dysphoria and violence. Obviously, the jury agreed.

69. What Do We Know About Serial Killers Who Use Poison? *(Germany)* For years, employees at a manufacturing business in the German town of Schloss Holte-Stukenbrock had been getting sick. So, when an employee noticed a strange white substance on his ham-and-cheese sandwich, it didn't take him long to alert his manager. To their credit, company personnel took his concerns seriously; they notified police and installed a surveillance camera in the break room.

What they discovered was horrifying. There on the video footage appeared quiet, unassuming 56-year-old machinist Klaus O (privacy laws in Germany prevent the last name from being published) taking his coworker's lunch out of the lunchbox, sprinkling white powder on the sandwich, and carefully rewrapping it and replacing it back in the communal refrigerator. The sandwich was quickly grabbed and the white powder sent for analysis. The mysterious powder turned out to be lead acetate, a toxic heavy metal that can cause organ failure and death. When police searched Klaus' home, they discovered a makeshift chemist's laboratory and a host of dangerous substances, including quicksilver, lead, and mercury. He was arrested on May 16, 2018.

No one had ever suspected Klaus of any malicious mischief. He had worked at the same company for thirty-eight years. Police suspect he may have poisoned as many as twenty-one employees over two decades while working at the factory, none of whom had any arguments or conflict with Klaus or any idea why they might have been targeted. A psychologist who evaluated Klaus after his arrest testified that Klaus didn't seem to have any personal animosity against any of his coworkers and said Klaus O "seemed to me like a scientist who was testing substances on a guinea pig."

In March 2019, he was sentenced to life in prison. The exact victim count—and his motive—may never be known and Klaus O did not speak at his trial. Sadly, his last victim, a 26-year-old, died in January 2020; he had been in a coma for four years.

The Psychological Profile of a Criminal Poisoner

So is Klaus O.'s quiet, unassuming demeanor typical of most poisoners? To date, little has been understood about the personality of the criminal poisoner. Part of this may be the skill with which many poisoners have eluded detection (it wasn't until the twentieth century that we were any good at detecting it). It may partly be due to stereotypes (females are more often portrayed as professional poisoners). Or it may be partly due to confounding variables (for instance, since poison is such an ideal weapon of choice, it may tell us more about the *intelligence* of the perpetrator than about their *personality*).

In some ways, Klaus O. was typical. Like most poisoners, he is a man. This surprises most people who assume poison is a woman's weapon. But contrary to popular belief, the majority of convicted poisoners are men, overwhelmingly so when the victim is a woman. When the victim is a man, the poisoner is equally likely to be male or female. As with other methods of murder, perpetrators rarely cross racial lines; neither did Klaus O. On average, a homicidal poisoner is five to ten years younger than his/her victim; we don't know how many people Klaus O. killed, but it appears his victims ranged in age from the early twenties and up.

But in other ways, Klaus O. was not typical. Career-wise, homicidal poisoners are over-represented in the medical or caretaking professions, where they have easy access to the means to kill and a bevy of vulnerable victims. Klaus, of course, worked in a valve factory; as a machinist, he did have access to a number of chemicals and was apparently eager to expand his arsenal of chemical weapons in his home laboratory. The majority of poisoners knock off someone they know, such as a child, spouse, friend, or acquaintance. While Klaus technically fits into this category (although he reportedly kept to himself and made no friends), a striking dissimilarity is Klaus' allegedly bizarre, and impersonal, motive.

Other than his quiet and reserved workplace persona, we don't know a lot about Klaus O.'s personality. Killing someone with poison requires planning and subterfuge, so it comes as no surprise that poisoners, as a group, tend to be cunning and creative (they can design the murder plan in as much detail as if they were writing the script for a play). They tend to avoid physical confrontation and, instead, rely on verbal and emotional manipulation to get what they want from others.

Convicted poisoners also tend to have a sense of inadequacy, for which they compensate through a scorn for authority, a strong need for control, wish-fulfillment fantasies, and a self-centered, exploitive interpersonal style. Often either spoiled as a child or raised in an unhappy home, some experts liken the poisoner's personality to an incorrigible child whose immature desire for their own way leads them to try to control and manipulate the world. It's as if the poisoner never grew up and is determined to take what they want as a child would from a candy store. Developmentally stunted, other people are viewed without empathy and the poisoner's internal compass is guided instead by greed or lust rather than morals. And, because poison is often not detected initially, the power and control poisoners experience with success tends to increase his or her confidence in future endeavors.

Typically, the motives are not much different from those in other homicides. Some poisoners revel in the role of tender, self-sacrificing attendant to the victim they are slowly killing; think of the cases like Jane Toppan and Dr. Harold Shipman (who killed at least 215 of his patients between 1975 and 1998), whose ministrations to their victims initially aroused tearful admiration and gratitude from family members. Some poisoners are more practical, bumping off relatives for life-insurance benefits or to speed along an inheritance. There are the rarer motivations for criminal poisoning, such as the aforementioned Munchausen by Proxy. Even Klaus O.'s motive is not unheard of; between 1962 and 1971, Graham Young killed at least three people, including his stepmother, and experimented on several more keeping a detailed diary of the dosages he administered his unwitting guinea pigs and the reactions he observed.

70. Has There Even Been Another Serial Killer Like the Tylenol Poisoner? (*Japan*) You may or may not be aware that we have a serial killer to blame for the fact that it takes the brains of a rocket scientist and the brawn of an Olympic body builder to get the cap off an aspirin bottle. Back in September 1982, seven innocent people (including a 12-year-old girl) in the Chicago metropolitan area lost their lives after taking extra-strength Tylenol for minor aches and pains. Someone had apparently slipped cyanide into random bottles on store shelves, so, for a brief period of time, taking Tylenol was the equivalent of playing Russian roulette. By early October, police had made the Tylenol link between these seemingly random deaths. Johnson & Johnson, the manufacturers of this now-deadly pain reliever, pulled thirty-one million bottles from store shelves and got to work making them tamper-proof.

No one was ever convicted for the poisonings although one man—James Lewis—sent an extortion letter to Johnson & Johnson, taking credit for the tampering and demanding one million dollars to prevent further deaths. He was quickly tracked down and arrested. An investigation soon revealed that, while Lewis might be a dirt-bag who was taking advantage of a horrible situation, he was not the actual poisoner. He was still sentenced to twenty years in prison for his criminal mischief and served twelve before his release. As of 2020, the thirty-eighth anniversary of the Tylenol poisonings, the case is still open and still unsolved.

The Japanese Vending Machine Murderer

In 1985, Japan had their own version of the Tylenol serial killer, but with a cultural twist. Between April and November of that year, in Hiroshima, twelve people died and thirty-five were seriously injured after consuming paraquat. Paraquat is a highly toxic weed killer (law enforcement often uses it to kill illegally-grown marijuana plants) that causes widespread damage to the kidneys, lungs, heart and liver; after an acute dose, death typically takes several days to approximately four weeks. No one in their right mind would ingest it willingly—and none of the victims did.

While it took police a while to figure it out, bottles of a popular vitamin-C enriched juice called Oranamin C—seemingly unopened—had been laced with paraquat and left in, or on top of, vending machines. At the time of the tampering, vending machines would sometimes give out two drinks instead of one as a good-will gesture and marketing ploy. Lucky and goodhearted recipients of the two-for-the-price-of-one drink would sometimes leave the second drink on top of the vending machine or still in the slot for the next thirsty customer to find. All of this stopped, of course, when the link between the drink and death was made. Like our homegrown Tylenol tamperer, the Japanese killer was never caught.

71. How Often Do Serial Killers Start Out as Rapists? ***(Australia)*** As most serial killers do, Bradley Robert Edwards pleaded not guilty to the three murders he was charged with in 2019; in September, 2020, he was found guilty of two. From the get-go, though, he admitted to two previous sexual assaults, including the rape of a teenage girl. This is not uncommon; many sexually-motivated serial killers were rapists before they "graduated" to serial murder. Before Joseph James DeAngelo was the Golden State Killer, he was the Eastside Rapist and is believed to have committed forty-five to fifty rapes. Samuel Little had been arrested dozens of times for numerous crimes, including assault and rape, before he began killing. Serial killer Anthony Sowell was a convicted rapist.

But what does this tell us? First of all, most rapists don't progress to murder. After all, aren't rapists a pretty diverse bunch? Isn't there a world of difference between the aggressive date who refuses to take no for an answer (or who interprets someone who is unable to say "no" as a "yes") and the serial rapist who creeps into a stranger's home?

Perhaps not as much as we once thought. A 2019 study of 12,624 college men across forty-nine campuses calls into question some common assumptions about date or acquaintance rape on campus, especially the idea that it's typically a one-time result of either a miscommunication between two people or is fueled by drugs or alcohol that cloud the judgment of an otherwise good kid who takes advantage of someone equally drugged or high. These researchers found that, while most college men do not take sexual advantage of another student under any circumstances, over 87 percent of alcohol-involved sexual assaults were committed by *serial perpetrators*. In other words, the majority of acquaintance rapes seemed to be less a result of a date *caught up* in the situation and more a result of a date *creating* those circumstances. Even more alarming, a select few continued on with their sexual assaults long after their college days were over, underscoring the importance of treating date rape seriously and intervening before there are more victims and the perpetrator's sexual proclivities progress. It also highlights the need to link serial sex offenses.

Unfortunately, our research shows that serial sex offenders are tricky; they often change the way they operate (for instance, starting out targeting females and moving on to couples), they are influenced by the situation (for example, whether a victim screams, tries to run, or is compliant), and they often choose victims based on opportunity rather than preference. But there is a glimmer of light at the end of the profiling tunnel. While it's still too early to draw any definitive conclusions, recent findings have indicated that many serial sex offenders have a pattern to their inconsistencies that we will eventually be able to predict how their crimes and crime scene behaviors—are likely to change over time. So, while (contrary to popular belief and unlike Clarice Starling from *The Silence of the Lambs*), we're not very good at profiling offenders, we may be able to profile crime scenes.

For the First Time, Two U.K. Serial Sexual Predators May Get Life Without Parole

In the United States, it's pretty rare for an offender who never killed anyone to get life in prison without the possibility of parole. In the U.K., it's unheard-of. However, that might soon change, thanks to two horrific serial rapists whose offenses were so heinous that the Attorney General's office has appealed their mandatory thirty-year sentences as "too lenient." These men are so dangerous, they argue, they should never again see the light of day.

They have nothing in common other than their predatory natures. Reynhard Sinaga, thirty-seven, is an Indonesian transplant who has been living in the U.K. on a student visa since age twenty-four. His father is a successful Indonesian businessman, who funded his son's multiple degrees and living expenses. People who knew him said he was friendly, openly gay, and well-liked; a former boyfriend as "kind and joyful." Others described him as harmless but vain and narcissistic, spending hours in front of the mirror taking selfies and grooming his hair. No one thought he was violent.

By night, however, Sinaga was a serial predator, luring intoxicated young men to his apartment (which was close to a number of bars) under a variety of pretexts; a place to charge their dead cell phone, somewhere to wait until a girlfriend showed up, an offer of another drink. Once inside, though, he would slip them GHB in a drink and sexually assault them, videotaping all of it. Between 2015 and 2017, he raped at least 195 men (each documented via video on his cellphone) and was convicted of raping forty-eight of them.

In contrast, thirty-five-year old Joseph McCann was English born, of Scotch-Irish descent, and heterosexual. He had a lengthy criminal history (theft, vandalism, burglary, mugging) trailing behind him when he engaged in a brutal two-week crime spree (April and May 2020) that involved raping eleven women and children; he broke into one home and forced one mother to watch him rape her teenage daughter and eleven-year old son. He snatched a twenty-one-year old woman off the street in broad daylight and raped a seventy-one-year old.

McCann and his two older brothers had a longstanding reputation as neighborhood bullies and he had first come into contact with police at age eleven. In fact, the hoodlums were so destructive that the family was eventually evicted from their home and the boys were banned from a Manchester suburb due to their antisocial behavior. He had only been out of prison for three months when his sexual assaults began.

72. Have There Been Young People Who Have Emulated Serial-Killing Relatives? ***(Australia)*** If you grew up Down Under, you'd probably prefer that your last name was not Milat. Back in the early 1990s, serial killer Australian Ivan Milat stalked, tortured, and killed seven young backpackers in the Belanglo State Forest just south of Sydney. He was incredibly sadistic, using some of his victims for target practice and occasionally severing their spinal cords so he would have them under his complete control. He was also a suspect in at least three other murders (and possibly many more) dating back to 1978. (He was convicted in 1996 and died behind bars of stomach and esophageal cancer in 2019).

This is not a family legacy most people would be proud of, but Matthew, Ivan Milat's great-nephew was enamored with it. He was only two years old when Uncle Ivan was arrested. Matthew never met his uncle, so it's hard to argue that Ivan was a bad influence. Nevertheless, as a teenager, Matthew not only idolized his infamous great-uncle; he began to use him as his role model. Seventeen years after Ivan Milat's seventh and final murder in 1993, Matthew returned to the same forest to kill his first (and, fortunately, only) victim.

Born as Matthew Meuleman, he grew up with his mother and stepfather in Bargo, New South Wales, a small town about sixty miles southwest of Sydney. Classmates described him as a quiet kid during his prepubescent years, someone who didn't stand out in a good or a bad way. But something steered him into a dark place in his early teens. at fourteen, he discarded his given surname and took on the infamous Milat. Some friends suggested that he did not get along with his stepfather and may have taken on the infamous surname out of anger.

On November 20, 2010, 17-year-old Matthew and two of his friends lured another mutual friend, David Auchterlonie, to the Belango State Forest. It was Auchterlonie's seventeenth birthday. Matthew and 19-year-old Cohen Klein had told Auchterlonie that they were going there to drink and smoke marijuana, but when they arrived, Matthew accused Auchterlonie of telling people that he had stolen money from his mother and of "spreading his business" around town.

Matthew tortured Auchterlonie while he pleaded for his life. He then killed him with a blow to the skull with a medieval ax. All the while, his friend Cohen Klein filmed the horrific events on his mobile phone. Another friend, Chase Day, stunned and allegedly in fear for his own life, tried to convince the two to stop but eventually helped drag Auchterlonie's body deeper into the bush to conceal him. The day after the murder, Milat was heard bragging about the murders, stating, "That's what the Milats do." Chase Day had had enough; he went to the police. Matthew Milat was sentenced to forty-three years in prison in 2012. He will be eligible for parole in November 2040. Cohen Klein received a thirty-two-year sentence, of which at least twenty-two must be served. While Day was initially charged as an accessory, the charges were eventually dropped.

73. Has There Ever Been a Cop Who Was a Serial Killer?
(Russia) It's scary to think that, among serial killers with a professional/governmental job, the top three professions have been police/security official, military personnel, and religious official. In other words, people in whom we place our trust. Members of this serial-killer-cop club include Soviet police officer Gennedy Mikhasevich (responsible for the death of at least thirty-three women between 1971 and 1985), former Miami cop David Stephen Middleton (three Nevada victims between 1993 and 1995), and German police officer Norbert Poehlke (who killed six people as part of a series of bank robberies in 1984 and 1985).

Few stand out like Mikhail Popkov, though. Popkov was a Russian police officer convicted of killing seventy-seven women over two decades (1992-2012). His killing career, he says, was triggered by his wife's suspected affair with a work colleague. Why Popkov thought serial murder was a better response than a divorce or couple's therapy is anyone's guess, but, for some abnormal reason, he decided instead to punish the "immoral" and "clean the city from fallen women;" in other words, he targeted innocent sex workers. Dressed in his police uniform, he would offer them a lift in his car and then drive them to a secluded spot in his hometown of Angarsk, Siberia, sexually assault them, and kill them with axes, knives, or screwdrivers. Some of his crime scenes were so gory that he was dubbed the "werewolf killer."

Because of the perpetrator's extreme violence, mental health professionals were sure they would find serious psychological problems in him when he was caught. (Thinking the amount of carnage at a crime scene is a measure of the perpetrator's mental illness is a common rookie mistake). Nope; not only did they find him free of any mental illness, they also found he had a remarkable memory for the details surrounding his crime.

Psychologists also quickly discounted his self-proclaimed twistedly altruistic mission of "cleaning up the streets." Instead, they cited his motive as "misogyny." In other words, he hated women and was looking for a reason to kill them. He was sentenced to life imprisonment in 2015 for twenty-two murders but has since confessed (with most of them verified) to fifty-nine more.

74. What Makes Someone Become a Cannibal? *(Russia)*

It's a given that if you're reading this book, you're not particularly squeamish. Even for diehard true-crime fans, though, this next story can be a little hard to swallow (pun intended).

Andrei Chikatilo, a.k.a. The Butcher of Rostov, grew up in the shadow of a terrible famine that hit Ukraine in the 1930s. Millions of people, including women and children, starved to death and rumors were that some citizens, out of desperation, resorted to cannibalism to survive. In fact, Chikatilo was often told that his older brother, Stepan, was kidnapped and cannibalized by neighbors when he was just four years old. Whether or not the story was true, this is not something a sibling needs to hear and mental health experts later wondered if this might have influenced Chikatilo's later culinary tastes.

Chikatilo's early life was rough in other ways. His father had been captured while serving in the Soviet army during World War II; this was viewed as "cowardice" by fellow villagers and reportedly brought shame and ridicule on the entire to the family. It also made the small and shy Chikatilo a target of school bullies. By the time he was a teenager, he was a bright but socially awkward student who had no skill with the opposite sex and was impotent during his few opportunities for romance. However, with the assistance of his sister's match-making skills, Chikatilo found a bride.

Despite Chikatilo's ongoing sexual difficulties, he and his wife also managed to have two children. Given his later sexual proclivities, part of Chikatilo's early sexual dysfunction may have been because he wasn't directing his sexual energies towards his true interests: children. In fact, his career as a schoolteacher was disrupted in 1973 when a string of complaints about sexual assaults on young children, forcing him to change schools several times.

Although never convicted for this crime, it is commonly thought Chikatilo killed his first victim, nine-year-old Yelena Zakotnova, in September, 1978. But his killing career began in earnest in 1981, after he was finally forced to quit teaching due to his sexual misconduct. He began befriending young runaways (boys and girls) at train stations and bus stops, luring them into nearby forest areas, where he would attack them, attempt to rape them, and mutilate them. In a number of cases, he ate the sexual organs or removed tips of their noses or tongues or other body parts. This truly put Chikatilo in a rare class as even serial killers typically don't eat their victims; out of every 2,000 serial killers, only five to ten will engage in cannibalism.

Chikatilo was caught when, on November 19, 1990, a police officer spotted him emerging from the woods with a streak of red on his check and a cut on his finger; the next day, the body of a young girl was found near the spot Chikatilo had been seen. Wondering if the two events might be connected, police brought him in for questioning. After a lengthy interview (nine days), he eventually confessed to fifty-six murders between 1978 and 1990, although only fifty-three could be verified. He was executed by a gunshot behind his right ear on February 14, 1994. He was fifty-seven.

What Do Cannibals Have in Common?

French scientists recently reviewed the medical files of five male patients ages 18 to 36 who had practiced pathological cannibalism, which they defined as cannibalism driven by psychological reasons (as opposed to, for example, to avoid starvation after surviving an airplane crash in a remote area or as part of a cultural ritual of eating the flesh of a dead loved one to take on his or her strengths). All of the patients had been hospitalized in a French psychiatric facility for at least twenty years.

Their first finding was that pathological cannibalism is *extremely* rare (thank God). When it does happen, it is most likely to occur among two types of individuals: those suffering from severe psychotic mental illness (most commonly, schizophrenia) and those experiencing extreme forms of paraphilia (sexual desires gratified by deviant activities) in combination with some kind of personality psychopathology. It also occurs against a backdrop of childhood trauma; all of the patients had dysfunctional childhoods that exposed them to sexual abuse, violence at home, or emotional neglect.

The two nonpsychotic patients admitted to cannibalistic fantasies or plans "going back many years," although feelings of humiliation seemed to be the trigger that prompted them to actually attack and eat their victims. Both reported that consuming the flesh of others relieved tension and soothed deep-rooted frustrations and enhanced their sense of self-esteem. The cannibalism was also accompanied by sexual acts involving the victims.

From a serial-killer perspective, Jeffrey Dahmer, Albert Fish, and, of course, Andrei Chikatilo fall into this category. For these killers, preparing the human meal was part of the ritual and taking such complete possession of their victims made them feel powerful and superior. Surely, the cannibal thinks, he is in a class all by himself. And, by consuming his victims, he will never be lonely again.

The three cannibals driven by psychosis were different. The cannibalism in the three schizophrenic patients typically followed a sudden outburst of violence. They murdered family members (typically parents) and then ate parts of their bodies. There was also a history of conflict and hostility in these parent-child relationships.

The authors concluded that the schizophrenic group used cannibalism as an extreme form of self-defense against a perceived physical or psychological threat. Joseph Oberhansley, an Indiana man accused of killing and eating parts of his forty-six-year old ex-girlfriend's body in 2014, was found incompetent to stand trial after his arrest. Thirty-seven-year-old Dwayne Wallick, who in 2020 was caught in the act of eating his 90-year-old grandmother, appears to also have been influenced by psychosis. And, last but not least, Richard Trenton Chase was a serial killer who, during 1977 and 1978, murdered six people and consumed their blood because he believed space aliens were turning his blood to powder. Chase is an interesting and complicated example of the interplay between psychopathy and psychosis; he appeared to have both.

75. What Country Recently Had Its First Serial Killer? ***(Cyprus)*** In June 2019, Greek-Cypriot army officer Nikos Metaxas was sentenced to multiple life sentences after confessing to the abduction and murder of seven immigrants between September 2016 and August 2018. His victims include five women and two children, six- and eight-year-old daughters of two of his adult victims, although investigators believe he may have killed up to thirty women. He met his victims on dating sites. He was caught after tourists accidentally discovered two of the women's bodies in early April 2019 and her internet history pointed to Metaxas.

Although at first Metaxas denied any involvement (how often have we heard that?), when faced with the evidence, he decided to try another approach. He then portrayed himself as a hero who wanted to set the (murdered) little girls free from sexual abuse perpetrated by male perverts as, he claimed, the mothers of the two young children were prostituting their children for money (there was zero evidence of this). By killing them, he insisted, he was really liberating them. Interestingly, Metaxas also killed three women without children, one of whom he strangled after she caught him filming their sexual encounter; I'm not sure how he was going to fit that into his narrative. He was also accused of raping an aspiring model.

From the moment the immigrant women were reported missing, calls for police to investigate fell on deaf ears. An internal probe after Metaxas' arrest showed that police often failed to take the missing person reports seriously; it further noted that the negligence was so overt that it could not be explained away by an excessive workload or innocent mistake, suggesting a more sinister explanation (such as racism). It also shed light on an exploitive immigration system where young migrant women work almost like modern-day slaves and have few rights or options.

There had also been a recent backlash against immigrants, which likely worked in Metaxas' favor. The Republic of Cyprus (the Greek part of the island) currently has the highest ratio of refugees to locals (one out of every five people) in all of Europe. It has historically been attractive and welcoming of immigrants. However, a 1991 pro-immigration law that made it easier for Cyprus to fill employment gaps has resulted in a huge influx of people from different nationalities, especially over the past four years. Some native Cypriots are now angry about it, blaming the immigrants they once welcomed for further tainting their ethnic heritage. Throw in an island already-divided between Greek and Turkish ethnicities, with the southern "Greek" part blaming its northern Turkish neighbors for allowing immigrants in and then encouraging them to migrate south, and you can see how the immigrants themselves could become scapegoats.

76. Has a Known Serial Killer Ever Gotten Away? ***(Hungary)*** Serial killer Bela Kiss took full advantage of World War I; in fact, you could even call it his ally. Because his last known victim was killed in 1914, it's hard to get a straight story about everything that happened. Still, what we think we know is too interesting not to be told.

In 1900, Bela Kiss was living in a small town outside Budapest and working as a tinsmith. He was twenty-three, good-looking, and relatively affluent. Unknown to those who know him, though, by 1903, he had already begun his criminal career, wooing women—especially widows—through marriage columns and personal ads, using the name

Hoffman and claiming to be a lonely widower looking for love.

It is unclear when he committed his first murder. At first, Kiss seemed to be content fleecing the unsuspecting women out of their money, somehow convincing them to turn their funds over to him and then finding a way to end the relationship. At least two of Kiss' victims—Margaret Toth and Katherine Varga (both murdered in 1906)—had attempted to sue Kiss to get their money back; this did not work out well for either one of them. In 1912, Kiss had married and discovered that his wife had been having an affair with the man who turned out to be his only male victim (along with twenty-three women). They were all eventually found stuffed and pickled in a barrel.

Kiss told his friends that his much-younger wife had run off with her new lover to America. It seems that wife's betrayal accelerated Kiss' killing career; many women disappeared from the Budapest region between 1912 and 1914. Around that time, police in the area noticed the seven large drums Kiss had on his property and suspected that he was manufacturing illegal alcohol. When questioned, Kiss insisted that he was hoarding gasoline to prepare for the upcoming world war. For some unfathomable reason, they accepted his explanation and left the drums untouched.

In 1914, World War I broke out and Kiss was either drafted or he enlisted. Given what he had concealed on his property, I'd guess the former. Before he left for battle, he padlocked the windows and doors to his house, and gave strict instructions to his housekeeper to disallow visitors and guard against trespassers.

There are conflicting accounts of what happened next. By 1916, no one had heard from Bela Kiss. At this point, either the lease on his house had run out and the owner had decided to repossess the house—or Kiss' previous story about keeping gasoline in the barrels had led to desperate attempts to obtain badly needed fuel for the war effort. Whatever the truth, the metal drums were opened and twenty-four bodies were discovered. A search of the house uncovered letters and a photo album suggesting that one hundred and seventy-five women had corresponded with Kiss and that he chose his victims based on their lack of family and vulnerability.

A manhunt began in 1916; since then, Kiss was reported as killed in action, wounded in battle, arrested on burglary charges in Romania, and dying of yellow fever in Turkey. In New York in 1932, he was allegedly spotted coming out of a New York subway. He was never captured and, if he has any more victims, we have yet to discover them.

Part 5: Modern-Day Serial Killers.

The dance between a serial offender and law enforcement is becoming more sophisticated. But while we seem to be catching serial-killer wannabes sooner, seasoned serial offenders may be getting smarter, at least about forensic evidence.

Some of the Serial killers Who've "Disappeared" in the 21st Century

Executed: Bobby Joe Long, Joseph Paul Franklin, Tommy Lynn Sells, Gary Ray Bowles, Yang Xinhai (China), Mohammed Bijeh (Iran), Matej Curko (Slovakia; killed in a shootout), Chen Ruiqin (Taiwan), Gabriel Wortman (killed in a shootout).

Suicides: Israel Keyes, Andrew Urdiales, Dale Hausner, Philip Markoff, Harold Shipman, John Wayne Glover, Javed Iqbal, Kam McLeod and Bryer Schmegelsky, Pazuzu Algarad, David Birnie, Volker Eckert, Oleg Zaikin, Pierre Chanal, Vlado Taneski, Jeong Nam-gyu (died from complications after failed hanging), Uwe Bohnhardt and Uwe Mundlos (Germany)

Killed by a Prison Inmate: Donald Harvey, Lenko Latkov (Bulgarian).

Died in Prison: Ivan Milat, Richard Ramirez, Lonnie Franklin, Jr., Charles Manson, Donald Harvey, Robert Hansen, Angus Sinclair (Scotland), Dominique Cottrez (France), Juan Corona, Phillip Jablonski, Robert Black (U.K.), Anthony McKnight, Dennis Nilsen (U.K.), Eddie Mosely, William J. Pierce, Jr., Lawrence J. Bittaker,, Roy

Lewis Norris, Richard Fran Biegenwald, Ernst-Dieter Beck (Germany), Rudy Bladel, Elfriede Blaunsteiner (Austria), Wayne Boden (Canada), Jerry Brudos, Carol Bundy, Angelo Buono Jr. (one of the Hillside Stranglers), Thomas Dillon, Edward Wayne Edwards, Walter E. Ellis, Viktor Fokin (Russia), Bobby Jack Fowler, Kendall Francois, Leonard John Frazier (Australian), Gerald Gallego, Billy Glaze, Jacquy Haddouche (France), Archibald Hall, Trevor Hardy (U.K.), William Heirens, Koos Hertogs (Netherlands), Colin Ireland (U.K.), Charles Jackson, Oleg Kuznetsov (Russia), John Ingvar Lovgren (Sweden), Orville Lynn Majors, William McDonald (born in U.K.; died in New South Wales prison), Sergey Maduev (Russia), Edward Mayrand, Raymond Leslie Morris (U.K.), Henryk Morus (Poland), Eddie Lee Moseley, Alvin Neelley, Donald Neilson (U.K.), Allan Patterson Newman, Clifford Olson (Canada), Anatoly Onoprienko (Russia), Yoni Palmier (France), Andras Pandy (Belgium), Derek Percy (Australian), Heinrich Max Pommerenke (Germany), Terry Peder Rasmussen, Ivan Roubal (Czech Republic), Sergei Ryakhovsky (Russia), Egidius Schiffer (Germany), Abdul Latif Sharif (born in Egypt, convicted in Mexico), Arthur Shawcross, Robert Yale Shulman, Daniel Lee Siebert, Darbara Singh (India), Valery Skoptsov (Russia), Vyacheslav Solovyov (Russia), John Straffen (U.K.), Peter Sutcliffe (U.K.), Serhiy Tkach (Ukraine), Ottis Toole, Vladimir Tushinsky (Russia), Ronald James Ward, Edward Delon Warren, Carl Eugene Watts, Peter Woodcock, Robert Zarinsky, Willem van Eijk (Netherlands).

Imprisoned: Bruce McArthur, , Richard Beasley, Michael Madison, Samuel Dieteman, Salvatore Perrone, Kelly Cochran, Samuel Little, Robert Hayes, Bradley Robert Edwards (Australia), Todd Kohlhepp, Donna R. Perry, Joanna Dennehy, Derrick Todd Lee, Brittany Pilkington, Chester Turner, Kori Ali Muhammed, James Fairweather, Anthony Sowell, Ryan Sharp, William Lester Suff, William Michael Gargiulo, Joseph James Deangelo, Mark Goudeau, Gilbert Chamba (Ecuador), Charles Quansah (Ghana), Reta Mays, Niels Hogel (Germany), Darren Deon Vann, , John Allen Muhammed and Lee Boyd Malvo, Vlado Taneski (Macedonia), Alexander Pichushkin (Russia), Robert William Pickton (Canada), Ronald Joseph Dominique, Viktor Sayenko and Igor Suprunyuk (Ukraine), Yoo Young-chul (South Korea), Jimmy Maketta (South Africa), Maxim Petrov (Russian), Chisako Kakehi (Japan), David Randitsheni (South Africa), Thozamile Taki (South Africa), Steven Gerald James Wright (U.K.), , K.D. Kempamma (India), Klaus O (Germany), Tamara Samsonova (Russia), Beate Zscape (Germany), Diane and Rachel Staudte, Oleg Wirth (Russia), Pavel Voitov (Russia), Inessa, Roman, and Viktoria Tarverdiyeva (Russia), Tsutomu Miyakazi (Japan), Futoshi Matsunaga and Junko Ogata (Japan), Takahiro Shiraishi (Japan), Yukio Yamagi (Japan), Michel Paul Fourniret (France), Aino Nykopp-Koski (Finland), Marcos Antunes Trigueiro (Bulgaria), Dellen Millard (Canada), Robert Lee Yates, Jr., Elizabeth Wettlaufer (Canada), Mohan Kumar (India), Motta Navas (India), Mikhail Popkov (Russia), Devendra Sharma (India), Very Idham Henyansyah (Indonesia), Yahya Farhan (Israel), Sonya Caleffi (Italy), Kenae Kijima

(Japan), Kaspars Petrovs (Latvia), George and Michel Tanielian (Lebanon), Juana Barraza (Mexico), Abdelaali Hadi (Morocco), Gracious David-West (Nigeria), Gilberto Ventura Ceballos (Panama), Krzysztof Gawlik (Poland), Antonio Luis Costa (Portugal), Jack Mogale (South Africa), Alfredo Galan (Spain), David Thabo Simelane (Swaziland; awaiting execution), Roger Andermatt (Switzerland), Yayuv Yagicioglu (Turkey), Levi Bellfield (U.K), Stephen Port (U.K.), Khalil Wheeler-Weaver, Juan David Ortiz, Peter Tobin (Scotland; England), Polatbay Berdaliyev (Uzbekistan), Nikos Metaxas (Cyprus), Andrea Volpe and Peitro Guerrieri (Italy).

Suspected Serial Killers (awaiting trial): Deangelo Martin, Lawrence Paul Mills, III, Samuel Legg, III, Brian Steven Smith, Robert Durst, Frederic Pechier (France), Sofia Zhukova (Russia), Neal Falls (killed by victim), Diego Ruiz Restrapo (Chile), Sunday Shodipe (Nigeria), Jollyamma Joseph (India).

77. Why Has the Number of Serial Killers Declined Over the Last Thirty Years? There is little disagreement that, since the 1970s, the number of serial killers has dropped. All kinds of numbers support this; for example, Mike Aamodt's serial-killer database indicates that 1989 was the heyday of serial killers with almost two hundred active predators at that time. Between 2010 and 2020, we've had forty-three.

The hypotheses as to why vary. Some researchers say it's because we Americans have wised up; we don't hitchhike and we guard our children more closely. Some say the spike in serial killers in the 1970s, '80s, and '90s was driven by cultural factors (for example, an increase in urban living, damaged soldiers and traumatized civilians who became parents after World War II). And then there are others who think we're just better at catching and keeping potential serial killers (better forensic techniques sentences, tighter parole, longer prison sentences) before they have a chance to ramp up. The bottom line is we don't know if there are fewer available victims, easier-to-catch criminals, or both.

78. Is Fame a New Motive for Serial Murder? Sure, there have been serial killers who sought media attention after they began killings; the San Francisco Zodiac taunted the police, Jack the Ripper pen-palled the newspapers, Dennis Rader contacted the news media and left a letter for the authorities at a local library. But the idea of fame as a *motive* for serial killing appears to be fairly new.

This appears to be at least part of Brendt Christensen's motivation for murder. Twenty-nine-year-old Christensen, a former University of Illinois doctoral student, lured international student Yingying Zhang (the young Chinese woman had only been in the U.S. for a month) into his car on June 9, 2017 as she waited for a bus. He then drove her to his apartment, forced her inside, and raped, choked, and stabbed her before beating her to death with a baseball bat. He then bragged to his girlfriend that he had killed twelve other people since 2001, calling Zhang victim "No. 13" and telling her that his killing spree began when he was nineteen.

Police are highly skeptical of Christensen's claims. For one thing, he researched murder extensively on his computer before he attacked Zhang, something you would not expect if killing was something he was used to. His girlfriend, Terra Bullis, who contacted the FBI after some of Christensen's claims and wore a wire for several weeks before his arrest, said the two of them attended a vigil for the murdered Zhang after her death and that he seemed proud as he bragged about how he'd killed others—even tracing "13" on her hand with his finger.

But, while his victim count is suspect, he clearly was a serial-killer wannabe who craved notoriety. He idolized past serial killers, especially Ted Bundy. His favorite novel was *American Psycho*, about a young serial killing professional who hunts at night. Most of all, he just wanted to be famous, texting his then-girlfriend two weeks before Zhang went missing that, "I don't care how I will be remembered, just that I am."

Amy Brown: Ms. Serial-Killer Wannabe

Apparently, serial killing is not strictly a male ambition. After her 2017 arrest, 24-year-old Amy Caroline Brown told local Washington state police she'd long fantasized about becoming a serial killer, describing herself as a psychopath whose homicidal thoughts began in middle school. She said murder was on her mind the instant she met her date through his personal ad on Craigslist. Not only was she going to kill him, she was going to rip out his heart and eat it.

Here was the victim's side of the story. The 29-year-old man said he placed the ad to try to meet people with similar interests after his therapist suggested he become more social. (The title of his ad was *Good Evening! Let's Go Zombie Hunting!)* The two initially met at a local bar, then walked around talking about their favorite shows and movies. Brown then asked the man if he wanted to have sex; he agreed and the pair decided to find a motel room since they both lived with their parents. After cuddling with clothes on for about ten minutes, Brown suddenly straddled her victim, announced she was a serial killer, and stabbed him in the chest. Luckily, he was able to overcome her and escape.

The motel clerk called police and 911. When officers arrived, they spotted Brown running across the motel parking lot and detained her. During her booking, they recovered a note in her pocket, reading, *"If you are wondering what I do with the heart ... I eat it. I will strike again."* During a search of her home, they found *Hannibal* DVDs (which she reportedly binge-watched), a journal outlining her plans to become a serial killer, and drawings for what she dubbed a "murder shack."

Brown eventually pleaded guilty and was sentenced to eighteen years after stabbing a man she met on Craigslist. I once contacted her to see if I could better understand what would lead someone to develop serial-killer ambitions. She told me that she didn't think an interview would be useful in terms of understanding budding serial killers because she has now realized her attempted murder was solely due to discontinuing her Abilify (medication commonly used to treat schizophrenia and other psychotic disorders). She said the only potential benefit to any conversation between the two of us was "to lobby for the company that makes the drug put a larger warning label on it." I am well aware that abruptly stopping an antipsychotic medication can have negative side effects, including a resurgence of psychological symptoms. But attempted murder is not one of them.

79. Have Mass Murderers Replaced Serial Killers? It's strange to think there might be trends in something like murder, but there does seem to be. Murder rates go up and down, the types of victims change, and so forth. Recently, some experts have proposed that mass murderers have become the new "serial killer" in terms of media attention and public fascination and believe that some mass murderers today would have chosen a serial killing career thirty years ago (and vice versa).

It *is* true that as serial killings began to slow down in the 1990s, mass shootings began to rise. At least in some cases, the perpetrators of mass shooters appear to fit the profile of someone who, in eras gone by, would be a serial-killer candidate. After investigating the 1999 Columbine shootings, for instance, FBI experts and consultants concluded that one of the shooters, Eric Harris, was the kind of psychopath who could easily have been a serial killer. The same has been said for Parkland shooter Nikolas Cruz, who had a long history of troubled behavior and violence and had a history of animal abuse. And mass murderers, like most serial killers, do tend to plan out their crimes.

But has the mass shooter *truly* replaced the serial killer? Are the kind of people who used to kill one person at a time, over a period of months or years, now choosing to grab a gun and go out in what they believe to be is a blaze of murderous glory? That's a tough question to answer.

For one thing, as we've already discussed, serial killers themselves are a diverse group. Other than their victim count of two or more, they don't always have much in common. Mass murder has the same kind of problem. There's disagreement among some experts as to how many people have to die in a single event before it's a "mass murder." And then there's the fact that some mass murderers, such as Elliot Rodger or Charles Whitman, first kill a family member before killing strangers in public. Is this domestic violence followed by mass murder or is it all part of the same event?

Also, just because serial killing has gone down and mass murder has gone up doesn't mean there's a connection between the two. It may be that serial killing has declined because it's harder to pull off, with mass murders reflecting a new type of killer, one often bent on revenge against real or representative people in response to a perceived injustice.

I could be persuaded that some revenge or mission-oriented serial killer in the 1970s might be a mass shooter today, but I don't think sexually-oriented serial killers like Samuel Little or Joseph DeAngelo would be satisfied shooting people with a gun. And what about those serial murderers with a money motive, like black widow Mary Elizabeth Wilson, who between 1955 and 1957, married and killed four husbands for their money? I'd need a lot of convincing to believe that the reason serial killing is down is *because* mass murder is up.

80. Has a Celebrity Ever Been a Serial Killer? Well, it depends on how far you want to stretch the definition of "celebrity." You won't find anyone who'd grace the cover of *People* magazine today. If you think of the nobility who ruled their lands with impunity hundreds of years ago, definitely. In 1762, Russian Countess Darya Saltykova was accused of torturing and beating one hundred and thirty-eight serfs (almost always young girls) to death. She was ultimately convicted of thirty-eight murders and spent thirty years in darkness and solitary confinement before she died. Gilles de Rais, a French military leader, baron, and compatriot of Joan of Arc, was executed in 1440 for the alleged sexual abuse and murder of over one hundred young boys. However, as early as 1443, there were murmurings of his innocence (he had angered the church prior to his arrest and his "confession" was obtained via torture) and, in 1992, he was posthumously exonerated by the French court.

Looking more at modern times, serial killer Rodney Alcala was a winning contestant on *The Dating Game* but didn't become famous until after his arrest. Skylar Deleon, convicted of killing three people and attempting to hire an assassin to take out his father and cousin, was a small-time child actor who appeared briefly on one episode of the *Mighty Morphin Power Rangers*. (Thank the Lord he wasn't the silver power ranger, Zhane, or my oldest son would never recover). And Robert Durst, while not exactly a celebrity, is a real-estate tycoon who has been accused of killing his first wife in 1982 as well as a female friend and confidante in December 2000. He was also acquitted of the murder of a neighbor in 2003.

81. Has a Celebrity Ever Been the *Victim* of a Serial Killer? Sharon Tate, famous actress and wife of film director Roman Polanski, who was murdered by Charles Manson's gang on August 9, 1969, is probably the only genuine celebrity. The next closest a celebrity has come to a serial killer is Ashton Kutcher. But not as a potential *victim;* as a potential *suspect.*

In May 2019, Kutcher testified at the trial of serial killer Michael Gargiulo (murdered at least three women between 1993 and 2008) as to how he had met victim Ashley Ellerin in December 2000 at a friend's birthday party. He was attracted to her, but, at that point, he had a girlfriend. By February 2001, though, they were both single, and on February 21st, the night of her murder, the pair had planned to go out.

Earlier that evening, Kutcher called Ellerin to let her know that he was running late. He suggested they skip dinner and just go out for drinks. She agreed and told him she was finishing up getting ready. He testified that he called her an additional three times to keep her updated on his schedule, leaving messages when she didn't answer her phone. He finally arrived at her house at 10:30 p.m., where he found the door locked and no one answering the door. Eventually figuring she had given up on him and gone out on her own, he left.

Ellerin was found dead the next day, stabbed forty-seven times only a few hours after Kutcher had last talked to her. Kutcher testified that, when he heard the news, he was "freaking out" because his fingerprints were on her front-door handle and he was terrified that he would be considered a suspect. He immediately contacted police to let them know.

Gargiulo, 43, was charged with two California murders in 2008 (Ellerin and another young woman) and, in 2011, an additional Chicago slaying. He has been described by prosecutors as a "serial sexual-thrill killer" who got pleasure out of watching and stalking his victims before he attacked them. He was convicted of the California murders in August 2019 and is currently on Death Row.

82. Have There Been Serial Killers Like Dexter Who Target Other Criminals? Pedro Rodrigues Filho, aka Killer Petey, isn't exactly Dexter, but he *is* a serial killer who killed other criminals. Described by one analyst as the "perfect psychopath," Filho went after other criminals and just about anyone else who had wronged him. He's responsible for at least seventy murders, ten of which he committed before he turned eighteen.

Filho's life got off to a bad start. He was born in 1954 in Minas Gerais, Brazil with a head injury as a result of a beating his father gave his mother while she was pregnant. His father continued the violent family tradition throughout Petey's childhood. By the time "Killer Petey" was a teenager, violence was second nature for him.

Filho committed his first murder in 1968, when he was just fourteen. The victim was his town's vice-mayor. The man had recently fired Filho's father, who was working as a school guard, for allegedly stealing food from the school.

Filho's father denied the allegations. In retaliation for his dad's termination, Filho shot and killed the vice-mayor in front of city hall. Filho then did his own "investigation" into the food-stealing allegations and murdered another school guard who was the supposed real thief.

After these two murders, Filho fled to Sao Paulo but carried his penchant for murder with him. He became involved in the drug trade, robbing drug houses and killing rivals. He fell in love with a woman named Maria Aparecida Olympia, who was soon killed by rival gang members; out for revenge, he tortured and murdered several gang members. During this time, he also killed his father, whose domestic violence towards his mother had eventually resulted in her death. Filho reportedly visited his father in jail, where he killed the older man by stabbing him twenty-two times and cutting out his heart, chewing it up, and spitting it out.

Filho was finally arrested in May 1973 (at age nineteen) and spent most of his adult life in prison, where most of his murders took place. While incarcerated, Filho appears to have appointed himself as something of a vigilante, meting out justice to inmates he believed deserved punishment; he committed at least forty-seven murders while he was doing time. One story has it that Filho was once placed in a police car for transport with two other criminals, including a rapist; by the time they got to their destination, the rapist was dead. He once told an interviewer that he enjoyed killing other criminals, especially with knives or blades. Although at one time his prison sentence reached four hundred years, he was released in 2007. Since 2018, he has had his own YouTube channel, which currently has over 150,000 subscribers.

Serial Killer or Something Else?

It can be incredibly frustrating to watch criminal after criminal escape justice. In Bangladesh, sexual assault is a crime where the perpetrator frequently gets away with it; only four percent of reported rape cases are ever prosecuted, and dozens of victims are killed. And it's getting worse; between 2018 and 2019, the number of sexual assaults doubled.

Many citizens are fed up. One, in particular, has apparently decided to circumvent the judicial system and take the matter into his own hands. In 2019, at least three rape suspects were found murdered. Each had a note hanging around their necks identifying them as a rapist, stating their death was their punishment, and warning other potential predators of a similar fate. In the last note, the killer identified himself as "Hercules."

The public response has been mixed; some have hailed this as-yet-unidentified killer as a hero and defender of women, while others warn against the potential lawlessness should citizens take the law into their own hands. Interestingly, some citizens believe that law enforcement officers are actually doing the killing, especially after some members of the Bangladeshi parliament publicly called for killing rapists in "crossfire."

"Crossfire" killings, which have been an unofficial but well-documented practice in the country's war on drugs, occurs when an accused criminal is taken into custody and then is killed by police in "self-defense" during a staged or nonexistent gunfight. So far, Bangladeshi police have strongly denied having anything to do with "Hercules" or the murdered men. But no one else has been arrested.

83. Is the Internet a Tool That Serial Killers Often Use to Find and Lure Victims? It depends on who you ask. Some critics say that social media is getting blamed for plain-old regular murders and some perpetrators just happen to recruit victims on the internet. All perpetrators meet their victims *somewhere* and we don't blame the place for what a person does; we wouldn't call a predator who lured a victim over the phone and then killed him a "telephone murderer." Don't forget that, long before the internet gave predators a new recruitment venue, serial killers like Nannie Doss (responsible for eleven murders between 1927 and 1954) were trolling for victims through lonely-hearts ads.

On the other hand, there is something special about the internet. Where else can you find so many people, quickly develop such a sense of intimacy, or, if you choose, engage in such widespread deception? Without a doubt, there is a difference between a quick telephone chat or bar pickup and someone who spends months luring a victim into a trap. Sure, most serial killers, like Richard Beasley, who lure their victims online would likely find another way without a computer. But the internet sure made it easier.

Beasley, a self-proclaimed street preacher and convicted felon, was not the kind of internet predator most of us worry about. He wasn't pretending to be a teenage boy so he could trick a young girl into sexual assault. He wasn't soliciting sex workers on the internet so he could torture and murder them. His vulnerable victims were middle-aged men who were down on their luck and willing to settle for a quiet life in the Appalachian hills of Ohio. In 2011, going by "Jack," he placed ads in the free-listings sections of Craigslist:

"*Wanted: Caretaker for farm. Simply watch over a 688-acre patch of hilly farmland and feed a few cows. You get $300 a week and a nice 2-bedroom trailer. Someone older and single preferred.*"

More than a hundred men applied and four were chosen, primarily because they had few family ties who might raise an alarm when they disappeared. Beasley, along with his 16-year-old accomplice, Brogran Rafferty, would encourage each victim to bring all of their worldly possessions (as they were allegedly moving in to a new home), meet the victim, buy him breakfast, and then, using a pretense (like a misplaced watch) stop at a remote location and shoot the victim.

Robbery and identity theft were his motives; he would steal, and sell, his victim's belongings and use their identities to claim Social Security benefits and apply for credit cards. He had also told his young accomplice that he needed another identity because he was "on the run" from some false criminal charges. Three were murdered; the fourth, forty-nine-year old Scott Davis, heard Beasley cock his gun just before he fired and managed to escape after being shot in the arm. Davis went straight to the police, who were initially skeptical of his story. But when they went back to the spot Davis had been taken, they found the grave of a previous victim as well as an open hole they believe had been prepared for Davis' body. In 2013, Rafferty was sentenced to life in prison and Beasley received the death penalty.

84. How Many Unidentified Serial Killers Are There (That We Know About)? How far back in time do you want to go? Of course, there's Jack the Ripper (five murders; 1888) whose identity, in spite of endless theories (and almost as many books), is still unknown. Austin, Texas had a serial killer who, in just a year (1884-1985), dragged eight innocent servants out of their beds and brutally executed them with a number of sharp objects (an axe, knife, cleaver, etc.) If you're an *American Horror Story fan*, you may remember the jazz musician-loving Axeman of New Orleans from season three; he killed six women between May of 1918 and October of 1919. The perpetrator behind the Cleveland Torso murders, five women and seven women between 1935 and 1938, has never been discovered.

But we don't need a time machine to find unsolved serial murders. Over the past half a century, there have been several series of murders that have been connected, either through forensic evidence or crime scene behaviors, but have not been solved. The Long Island serial killer (bodies of eight young women who worked as sex workers and advertised on Craigslist were found in 2010, along with a man dressed in women's clothes and a toddler whose mother was also a victim), is still an active investigation as is the San Francisco Zodiac (who murdered at least five people in the San Francisco Bay area in 1968-69). Also, in San Francisco, between January 1974 and September 1975, up to fourteen gay men were sexually assaulted and murdered by "the Doodler;" the unknown serial killer earned his nickname because he charmed his victims with drawings of them before luring them to their death. There was also the Freeway Phantom. His reign of terror in Washington D.C. began in April 1971 and suddenly stopped seventeen months later and after six young African American girls were killed. In spite of numerous tips and leads, his identity remains a mystery. There have been the Redhead Murders (6-11 victims; 1978-1992), the Gypsy Hill Killings (5 young women; 1976), and the Alphabet Murders (3 victims; 1971-1973). And, sadly, the list goes on.

There have been other suspected series that have not been publicly acknowledged by law enforcement. For example, over the last twenty years, Chicago has had a series of strikingly similar strangulation murders. Since the first victim was found in 2001, numerous bodies of sex workers or women with a history of drug addiction have turned up in empty lots, vacant buildings, dark alleys, and even garbage containers ever since then. Recently, in cooperation with the Chicago Police Department, the FBI has been investigating over fifty of these unsolved murders, in an attempt to find out whether they might be the work of one—or more—serial killers.

We aren't the only country that has trouble catching the bad guys; Italy has never conclusively identified the Monster of Florence, responsible for the murder of eight young couples between 1968 and 1985. There are unsolved serial murders in many countries: Namibia, Belize, Singapore, Sri Lanka, Costa Rica, Columbia, Portugal, and just about anywhere else you can throw a dart on a map.

Is There a Smiley Face Killer?

The Smiley Face Killer theory is one of the most controversial explanations for why forty-five bodies of young, drunk, college-aged men have been found floating in rivers across eleven states since 1997. Proponents of this theory, primarily two retired New York detectives and a criminal justice professor, believe there is a serial killer, or a gang of them, who target these young men, secretly drugging them with a "date rape" drug while drinking in a bar and then murdering them in a way that is staged to resemble an accidental drowning. Smiley Face graffiti has been found near twenty-two of the bodies.

In 2008, the FBI took a look at the alleged cluster and concluded there was no evidence of foul play and likely no serial murderer. They believe these are random alcohol-related drownings and the smiley faces, when present, are dissimilar to each other and appear to have been created at various times in relation to the victims' deaths; some are old and faded and could have been there for years. In 2010, the nonprofit Center for Homicide Research posted a similar opinion.

Still, there are those who say that the profiles of the victims are amazingly similar, and, in some cases, there has been evidence of trauma prior to death as well as toxicological evidence of a date-rape drug. What do you think?

Part 6: Serial-Killer Friends, Families and Fans.

How could a spouse not suspect that her husband was seriously disturbed? Do serial killers love their children? And why do some seemingly normal people fall in love with them *after they've been convicted*? The relationships serial killers have with the people around them can vary from partners-in-crime to innocent family members who wind up feeling guilty by association.

85. Why Are We So Fascinated by Serial Killers? As I said in the introduction to this book, this is something I've thought about a lot, given my chosen profession. It's hard to fully answer this question for myself, even harder to understand why so many other people are interested in it. I'm not the only one who has wondered about our fascination with true crime. Which, by the way, is nothing new. Serial killers and other bad guys have attracted attention since the rise of mass-circulation newspapers in the early nineteenth century. In fact, I could write a book on the theories behind our culture's fascination with serial killers; some people actually have!

Some of the most popular theories are:

- **We're curious about people who seem like us but aren't.** The crimes of serial killers are frequently monstrous. But, in everyday life, many of the murderers themselves are able to blend in, are outstanding role-players, are adept at appearing normal. They have families, jobs, and appear to be functioning members of the community. They are sons, daughters, husbands, and wives. Essentially, they fool everyone around them. I think it is this discrepancy between how serial killers appear and how they really are that is so compelling. It is horrifying—and fascinating—to think that a person capable of such atrocities can be hiding in plain sight.

• **We want to recognize danger so we can avoid it.** There's an Irish proverb: "Better the devil you know than the devil you don't." While it can be scary to learn about the horrible things people do—and have done—it can be empowering to understand the motivations, emotions, and actions of dangerous people. Why? Because this can help us figure out what people and situations to avoid, and how to spot, and report, something that doesn't seem right. As a crime writer, I've often been amazed at the safety tips my readers share. And, while no one thinks interfering in a police investigation is a good idea, everyday citizens who've spoken up have prevented suicides, solved missing-persons cases, and, by providing useful information to law enforcement, brought killers to justice.

• **We want to experience the danger without being at risk.** Just as horror movies allow us to experience fear and excitement from a distance, reading about convicted serial killers allows us to experience the adrenaline rush of fear without ever being in harm's way. It's cathartic; we experience uncomfortable emotions in a controlled way, knowing there will be justice in the end. In some ways, it's similar to our need to look at car accidents, train wrecks, or natural disasters; we might feel guilty looking, but it sure is hard not to.

• **We think serial killers are "cooler" than they really are.** Contrary to some expert opinions, I don't think the media glorifies serial killers. But I do think they sometimes sensationalize them in order to tell a good story. Any good fiction writer will

> tell you that, unless your readers can sympathize with the "bad guy," they won't continue reading. So, they work to make him human; they show his tragic upbringing, they attempt to explain why he does the bad things he does, they imply regret or remorse for past misdeeds. This same strategy with true crime, though, can have unintended consequences; callous serial killers who tortured innocent victims can come across as misunderstood and attractive-but-evil geniuses.

One interesting tidbit to consider is that our interest in serial killers is not only driven by who the serial killer is or what they did but also who *we* are. A 1995 study on why adolescents watch horror films found that "gore-watchers," viewers who liked the blood and guts, tended to have low levels of empathy and a strong need for adventure-seeking. "Thrill-watchers," who used movies to get the adrenaline rush of being scared, had high levels of adventure-seeking but also high levels of empathy. Gore-watchers tended to identify with the killer, while thrill watchers tended not to identify with killer or victim; they were captivated by the suspense. While true crime is different than fiction, I imagine our individual psyches also shape our interest in serial killers.

86. What is Murderabilia and What are the Ethics of It? True-crime murderabilia is the term used to describe the buying and selling of objects connected with violent crimes; the items often come from the perpetrators themselves. Collectors can buy items such as John Wayne Gacy's Pogo the Clown paintings (he used to volunteer at various charities dressed up in a clown suit), a lock of Charles Manson's hair, or Ted Bundy's Christmas card. It is a big business; Gacy's last painting is listed for sale at $45,000.

As you can imagine, this business has its detractors. What's so special about something just because it was once owned by a violent criminal? Why should anyone be able to profit from their crimes? And what about the victims? Imagine what it would feel like to be a family member of a serial killer's victim and know that he was profiting off your loved one's pain. Victims' activists like former parole officer Andy Kahan are fierce crusaders against the sale of these items. Eight states have passed Notoriety for Profit laws, which outlaw anyone from profiting off of similar items. In 2001, Ebay banned the sale of these items on their site under its policy on offensive materials.

Of course, there are two sides to every argument (although I admit I fall squarely in the "let's ban memorabilia" camp). Memorabilia dealers argue that they are simply preserving a piece of history and that it's no different than keeping a piece of rubble from one of the downed 9/11 towers or having a picture of Lincoln assassin John Wilkes Booth. Collectors are surprisingly diverse, running the gamut from the truly creepy (who were likely drawn to this dark hobby because of their own unrealized fantasies) to everyday true-crime fans to criminal-justice professionals whose "trophies" represent law-enforcement victories. Some people even believe these artifacts have supernatural powers, providing protection or granting special abilities to their owners, although, of course, there is zero evidence this is true.

87. How Many Serial Killers Work in Teams? When we think of a serial killer, we typically think of one person. For obvious reasons, most serial killers *do* work alone; coordinating murderous activities while evading capture is hard work. But it happens; more than a fifth of serial killers operate in teams, most often two people who are killing together. When we're talking about *female* serial killers, the percentage goes up to a third. The power dynamics between the couples vary from a dominant-submissive relationship to equally enthusiastic partners-in-crime. Occasionally, there have been serial killing groups, typically either a family working together or a destructive cult whose members kill at the behest of their leader.

As you can see, team serial killers are as varied as their solo compadres. However, when we compare solo serial killers as a group to those who work in teams, some overall differences emerge. Team killers tend to get caught sooner (most commonly killing for only a year before arrest in comparison to three years per solo killer) but kill more victims (four, in comparison to an average of three victims per solo killer).

They also tend to kill for different reasons. The most prominent motive for solo killers was enjoyment; this makes sense, as what gives us sexual pleasure, excitement, or a sense of control are highly individualized. Team serial killers were more often motivated by money. These different motives likely influenced how each group murdered, with team serial killers choosing less personal (and quicker) murder weapons such as a gun or poison; if the murder is a means to an end (money), it makes sense to get it over with as fast as possible. On the other hand, if the serial killer is motivated by the sadistic process itself, then stabbing, beating, or choking someone to death might be part of the fun.

The Dynamics of Deadly Duos

We typically think about mixed gender killing teams when we think about deadly duos. There have, however, been a number of same-sex pairs whose bond seems to center around depravity. Most of these were not romantically involved.

Delfina and Maria de Jesus Gonzalez were two sisters who owned and operated a Mexican brothel named Rancho El Angel in the early 1960s. Lots of people died there. Customers disappeared if they acted up or bothered the girls; they also vanished if they showed up with a wallet full of cash. "Sex workers" were killed, employees were murdered. No one was immune.

Clearly, this was not a typical brothel. Many of the "sex workers'" were actually innocent girls who thought they were being hired as housemaids, only to discover the truth once they arrived at Rancho El Angel; some of the girls were actually kidnapped. Once there, the girls had nowhere to go. They were subjected to unimaginable horrors: forced abortions, torture and/or murder if they lost their looks, got sick, or failed to please the customers. Drugs were readily available and, if the girls weren't forced to use cocaine or heroin (which sometimes happened), the drugs were strategically used to get the girls hooked so they could be exploited.

Rancho El Angel was finally raided by the Mexican government in 1963, at which time the bodies of eleven men and eighty women were discovered in shallow graves; investigators eventually linked the sisters to ninety-one murders. Tried in 1964, the Gonzalezes were sentenced to forty years each; two other sisters received shorter prison sentences.

While Maria and Delfina shared a biological bond, other serial killing pairs bonded over mutual interests. Leonard Lake met Charles Ng in 1981 after he posted an ad in a war-gamers magazine. By this time, Lake had engaged in a number of criminal activities, including the murder of Lake's brother and his best friend. Interestingly, Lake was trolling for victims when he met Ng and, the realization that he had met someone who had equally sexually deviant desires and lack of moral compass changed the nature of their relationship. Together, they murdered somewhere between eleven and twenty-five Californians between 1983 and 1985 before they were arrested.

88. How Do Team Serial Killers Decide to Work Together? Typically (but not always), one person in the serial-killing team is the driving force behind the serial murders. The dominant partner typically already has a history of deviant fantasies or criminal behavior before teaming up with someone who is vulnerable, either because of their insecurity, youth, neediness, mental instability, or lower intelligence.

It's often uncanny how the leader of a serial-killing duo seems to be able to spot a partner who is willing to give him or her whatever he wants. So how does the budding serial killer do it? Once the driving partner hones in on a potential collaborator, they set up a test.

The recruiter might share deviant sexual fantasies or extremist ideas to see how his potential recruit responds. Paul Bernardo asked Karla Homolka to participate in increasingly extreme sex acts; together, the two of them murdered three teenage girls between 1990 and 1992 (one of the victims was Homolka's sister). Homolka was not Paul Bernardo's first recruit; he apparently followed a pattern with several young women he dated. Initially, he would be attentive, generous, and caring. He would win over the girl's family. It was only when he thought he had her wrapped around his finger that he began to control and abuse her.

Other girls had failed the test. They got scared and ended the relationship, but not Homolka. She reacted by becoming fully compliant, willing to do whatever Bernardo asked of her. On top of that, as his abuse grew, she lost confidence and became even more dependent on him.

Ian Brady used another strategy. Before they murdered five children in the 1960s, he spent months indoctrinating 18-year-old Myra Hindley with his supremacist ideology, at one point, he even involved her in a fake burglary to test her loyalty to him. When she passed that test, he knew he had found his woman.

However, it's more complicated than the innocent sheep meeting big bad wolf. While one partner may not have started the serial-killing ball rolling, there are often pre-existing signs that the non-dominant partner was missing a scruple or two. Before she ever met Paul Bernardo, Karla Homolka had bullied people she thought looked "weird" and once shrugged off a failed experiment that resulted in the death of a friend's hamster. After her arrest, she cut a sweet deal with prosecutors in exchange for her testimony against Bernardo; luckily for her, the deal was signed before they watched the couple's home videos, which showed just how actively Homolka had participated in the murders.

Who Was the Real Mastermind?

In January 2020, 57-year old Catherine Wood was paroled after spending thirty years behind bars. She and her romantic partner and coworker, Gwendolyn Graham, had been convicted of killing five nursing-home residents at the Old Alpine nursing home in Walker, Michigan in 1987. They were arrested after Wood told her ex-husband about the murders in 1988 and he contacted the police.

Wood said that she and her lover started out playing pranks on the job, such as randomly moving patients from room to room, confusing other staff and the residents themselves, many of whom had dementia. They then thought it would be fun to kill patients whose first names would eventually spell out the word "murder." When this proved to be too difficult (some of the chosen alphabet-chosen victims proved too strong to subdue), they decided to incorporate their murder count into their love language. So, after the first murder, they would tell each other "I love you forever and a day;" after the fifth, "I love you forever and five days."

During the trial, Wood testified that she was just the lookout during the murders and it was Graham doing the killing. She also said that the murders were Graham's idea and they were done "for fun" and to seal their bond. Graham, who is serving life in prison without the possibility of parole, tells a different story. From the time they were arrested, Gwendolyn Graham has insisted that no one was actually murdered (dying, instead, of natural causes) and that Wood made up the entire story to get revenge on her after she cheated on Wood with another woman.

We may never know exactly what happened or who was in the driver's seat. It's hard to imagine confessing to being an accomplice to murder, no matter how angry you are at your cheating partner. True-crime writer, Lowell Cauffiel, who wrote a 1992 book about the case, and retired police sergeant, Roger Kaliniak, both believe that Catherine Wood was the real puppet master behind the murders and that Gwendolyn Graham was the puppet.

89. Has a Team Serial Killer Ever Killed His Partner?

Yes. Two come to mind. The first is Dean Corll, a Houston-based serial killer whose nickname was the Candy Man because of his family's candy factory and the fact that he often handed out free candy to local children. In August 1973, he was murdered in his own home by his serial-killing accomplice, Elmer Wayne Henley. Prior to this, Corll, with Henley and another accomplice, David Brooks, lured unsuspecting teenage boys to Corll's lair and had raped, tortured, and murdered twenty-seven of them.

Henley and Brooks had been willing to do anything for Corll; he had befriended them as young teenagers and both saw him as a father figure. He also paid them $200 for each adolescent boy they delivered. Even though both knew what Corll was doing with these children, they looked the other way, and, on several occasions, even delivered friends of theirs right into his hands. But when it came down to a personal matter of life and death, one accomplice finally drew the line.

By the summer of 1973, accomplice Brooks had married his pregnant girlfriend and moved away. Henley was still hanging around but increasingly wary of Corll, who had shown an interest in Henley's younger brothers. Then, on August 8, Henley showed up at Corll's house with his new girlfriend and a male buddy. Corll, who was strictly into same-sex activities, was furious.

According to Henley, after he and his friends passed out from partying, Corll put them in restraints. When Henley sobered up, he was terrified; he knew what was coming. Somehow, though, he convinced Corll to let him loose; it would be a lot more fun, he said, if the two of them killed the others together. After some convincing, Corll freed Henley, who immediately shot him to death, freed the other two, and called the police. Henley later confessed to his involvement in at least eight murders. He has been in a Texas prison for the past forty-seven years.

This next story is an example of there being no honor among thieves (or, in this case, murderers). Serial killer and contract assassin Richard Kuklinski estimated that he has killed between one hundred to two hundred and fifty victims. Most of the killings were contract hits for organized crime. Some, though, were for personal reasons and a few were for no reason at all.

Both Kulinski and his partner, Robert Pronge, had a lot in common. They were both hired assassins. They both had cool nicknames; before he was caught, Kuklinski was known as the Iceman because he would freeze his victims for months and then defrost the corpses and leave them to be found in a public place. Kuklinski's partner, Pronge, was nicknamed Mr. Softee because he used an ice-cream truck to freeze and transport his victims. In spite of their commonalities, though, they both became increasingly paranoid as they worked together, with each one worried that the other knew too much. Things came to a head on August 10, 1984, when Kuklinski eliminated Pronge with a single shot to the head.

90. How Much Do Female Team Members Participate in Murder with a Male Cohort? As we've already discussed, there is wide variability in the power dynamics between a male-female serial killing team. Yes, there are female partners who are either willing to throw the victims under the bus to keep a man happy or are unwilling sidekicks too afraid to stand up to a violent man. But a closer look at some serial-killing teams shows that one was like a stick of dynamite and the other a match; putting the two together ignited the explosion. There are women who, once they hook up with a bad man, feel free to indulge in some of the same sadistic activities we typically see in solo male serial killers. And don't forget, the power dynamics can change.

Charlene Williams, for example, didn't have the same shady background before hooking up with husband-to-be Gerald Gallego (he was the son of the first man executed in the Mississippi gas chamber and had seven felonies under his belt by the time he was in his early thirties). But she was quick to get over any scruples she might have had. On September 12, 1978, almost a year to the day after Williams met Gallego, she participated in the kidnapping, rape, and murder of two young girls. Two months before that, she had had a foursome with his fourteen-year-old daughter and young teenage friend.

It does seem that Gallego subjected Williams (who later became Ms. Gallego after the two married) to physical and psychological abuse. But it also seems evident that Williams willingly lured young girls for Gallego, had her own affairs in spite of Gallego's disapproval, and on at least one occasion, shot at him after he began sexually abusing girls without her. Williams denied ever killing any of the victims and struck a plea deal after their arrest. After her release from prison in 1997, she portrayed herself as a battered spouse who was unable to stop her evil husband from committing his dastardly deeds. I doubt it.

91. Has There Ever Been a Serial-Killing Family? Yep. Throughout time, there have been families who robbed and murdered as a way to make a living, giving a new meaning to the term "family business." The Wild West of the 1800s, in particular, seems to have had more than its share of families bound together by criminal activity. The "Bloody Benders," for example, was a diabolical family of four who would rob and murder weary travelers who stopped at their Kansas tavern in the 1870s. Ten years later, the Kellys turned up, a family of five from Kansas who murdered eleven travelers.

And then, there's the Sawney Bean clan. If any of this legend is true, this 16th century Scottish tribe is in a class of its own. The historically-unverified-but-horrifying story paints a picture of a group of incestuous, cannibalistic connivers who lived in a cave and targeted passersby for finances and food. Most scholars believe there was no real Sawney Bean, but that the story may sprung from a real-life character, Christie Cleek, a fourteenth century butcher-turned-robber who was known to slice off and eat a piece of meat from one of his victims.

Fast forward to contemporary times and you uncover the Russian Tarverdiyevas who, between 2007 and 2013, robbed and killed at least thirty people. No one knows why a former nursery schoolteacher and her dentist husband would ditch their day jobs and decide to include their two daughters in a criminal career that involved pretending to go on family camping trips and then murdering fellow campers. When arrested, mom Inessa compared the family's criminal routine to anyone else's daily trip to the office; i.e., it was a way to make a living.

Born Into Evil

It could be argued that Seema Gavit and Renuka Shinde never had a chance at living a law-abiding life. Their mother, Anjana Bai Gavit, had been arrested for one hundred and twenty-five counts of petty theft in her native city of Pune, India by the time her youngest daughter, Seema, was born; at the time, Renuka was just four years old. Both girls soon learned to steal at their mother's knee. However, it is likely that this family would have remained just a den of thieves if not for two events.

Anjana's first husband deserted her shortly after she gave birth to their daughter, Renuka; desperation was the likely reason she started pickpocketing for a living. But when her second husband, Mohan, did the same thing, leaving Anjana with four-year-old Renuka and newborn Seema, Anjana's heart permanently hardened. For Anjana, there was no turning back.

Anjana was hellbent on revenge against the spouses who deserted her. In 1990, when Seema was nineteen and Renuka was twenty-three, Anjana ordered her girls to kidnap their new half-sister, Kranti, Mohan's daughter by his new wife; she then murdered the girl. Around this same time, Renuka was caught pickpocketing at a local temple and was immediately surrounded by an angry mob. Thinking on her feet, Renuka pointed to her toddler son insisting that no mother would commit a crime with a child in tow. The ruse worked and Renuka was freed. But this event had planted a horrible seed; why not always take a child along as a foil? And why put your own child at risk when there were so many poor children at your disposable?

Over the next six years, up to forty children were kidnapped. The lucky ones were let go after they served their purpose. Some were deliberately hurt to create a distraction; once, when Seema was caught by a man whose wallet she was trying to steal, Anjana threw a child on the ground so hard that it caused a head injury. Seema slipped away as onlookers gathered around the hurt child. Any child who caused problems (cried "too much" or talked about his parents) or outlived his or her usefulness was doomed; at least nine children, including a nine-month-old baby and an 18-month-old toddler, were murdered.

In the end, it was Anjana's vengefulness that toppled the trio's criminal careers. In November 1996, Anjana hatched a plot to kidnap and murder Mohan's second daughter. (This woman could really hold a grudge). Fortunately, Mohan's new wife contacted the police and all three women were arrested. They were eventually charged with thirteen kidnappings and nine murders of children under age five between 1990 and 1996. The two sisters are currently on death row; Anjana died a year into her prison term. If they are executed, they will be the first Indian women put to death since 1955.

92. Could Someone Fall in Love with a Convicted Serial Killer? It's one thing to marry a man who turns out to be a murderer; it's another to marry someone you already know is one. But it happens. In some cases, women have even left happy marriages, thriving children, and satisfying careers, all for the love of a condemned man. In 2015, for example, married prison seamstress Joyce Mitchell was arrested after falling for an inmate at Dannemora prison in upstate New York and assisting him and his friend escape by hiding a hacksaw in some hamburger meat. She was supposed to meet the men with a getaway car after they successfully sawed their way out of prison but had a change of heart after it occurred to her that the convicts might kill her husband (also an employee at the prison) once she picked them up. One of the escaped men was shot dead after his escape; the other was also shot but managed to survive. Mitchell served four years in prison for helping them escape and was released in February 2020.

Many of these women are neither dumb or naïve. One of the most famous is Rosalie Bolin, a Miami socialite and paralegal who abandoned her criminal defense-lawyer husband and four young daughters to marry serial killer Oscar Bolin. They were married from 1996 until he was executed in 2016. Prison psychologists have had affairs with inmates; in Australia, for instance, a psychologist who worked with sex offenders lost her ability to practice after she became romantically involved with a member of a child-rape gang. Don't underestimate how charming and seductive predators can be, even from behind bars; these women knew better but fell for it anyway. There are some people, primarily women, who are attracted to serial killers *because* of their crimes, not in spite of them. Psychologists even have a name for it: hybristophilia, a sexual attraction to offenders who have committed violent crimes such as rape or murder. In a minority of cases, the affinity may be a chance to vicariously experience violence; in other words, from a personality perspective, some of these women may be a lot like the inmates themselves. Studies looking at psychopathic personality traits found that female college students who scored higher on psychopathic traits were more likely to be romantically attracted to psychopathic men.

Of course, there are many motives driving serial-killer groupies. Some seek to share the spotlight of their infamous partner. Some think they can change or save them. And some enjoy the intense-but-distant courtship without any of the real-life responsibilities or demands; imagine the amount of affection and attention you could get from someone who spends twenty-three hours a day behind bars.

Read This Before You Write to an Inmate

Carol Spadoni met Philip Jablonski when he put an ad for a pen pal in a local newspaper. At the time, he was in prison for the 1978 second-degree murder, assault, and attempted rape of his second wife. Correspondence blossomed into courtship and, in 1982, while he was still incarcerated in San Quentin, Spadoni married him.

However, during prison visits over the years, Spadoni became increasingly alarmed, telling a friend he was "weird" and that she was starting to be afraid of her husband. By the time he was paroled in 1990 (despite having tried to strangle his mother with a shoelace during a 1985 visit), she wanted nothing to do with him; shortly before he was let out, Spadoni told a friend that she was afraid of her husband and wanted to end their relationship.

Spadoni tried to protect herself and her mother, who lived with her. She talked with his parole officer about her fears and concerns. The officer tried to help; not only was Jablonski forbidden to travel to Burlingame, California (where Spadoni and her mother lived), he was not allowed to travel more than fifty miles from his residence in Indio, California without getting special permission from the officer. Spadoni also gave the possessions she had stored for Jablonski to one of his friends so she would not have to see him at all once he was released. Jablonski's friend passed the possessions and the message along.

None of this helped. On April 22, 1991, Jablonski drove to Spadoni's house, where he raped, tortured, and murdered her and her 72-year-old mother. Law enforcement also discovered that, during the short time he had been paroled, he had murdered two other women, including a fellow community college student whom he had offered a ride. In 1994, he received the death penalty. He died on death row in San Quentin prison in December 2019.

93. What is It Like to Grow Up with a Parent Who is a Serial Killer? There are really two parts to this question. One is what it would be like for your mother or father to be arrested as a serial killer while you're still a child. The second is what kind of upbringing a serial killer is likely to provide their own children.

Most of the children of serial killers who have spoken out found out about their parents' crimes as an adult. So, we don't have a lot of firsthand accounts of what life would be like for a child whose serial-killing parent was captured while she was growing up. I imagine the other parent might move to another city, change the family name, and hide any kind of relationship as much as possible; it's hard to imagine what kind of family conversations you'd need to have to explain all of that.

Almost all of the family members, who were themselves innocent of any crime, struggled. Some have stayed under the radar as much as possible. Some have written books, become victim's advocates, and reached out to support others in similar circumstances as they've come to terms with it over the years. No matter how they've coped, many of the adult children say they have dealt with shame, stigma, and guilt by association, yet another reminder of just how diverse a serial killer's victims are.

The second question, how serial predators parent their own children, is more complicated. While many of the killers were surprisingly similar as perpetrators, they were surprisingly different in their roles as Mom or Dad. Some were doting and some were dangerous. Mae West, daughter of serial-killing couple Fred and Rosemary West (and, of course, not the famous actress/movie star), has spoken openly about the physical and sexual abuse she suffered at her parents' hands. Two of the couple's victims were Mae's siblings. She's also talked about the discrimination and stigma she experienced as an adult because of her parent's crimes.

Others weren't directly abused but certainly knew something was off. Melissa Moore, daughter of serial killer and truck driver Keith Hunter Jesperson (who killed eight women in the early 1990s), recalls her dad as attentive and kind whenever he would come back from a trip. But she also remembers him torturing little kittens she found in the cellar of their farmhouse when she was five and laughing as she cried and pleaded with him to stop.

Yet others were completely blindsided to learn that the loving father who attended soccer games had a dark side that they never imagined. Matthew Ridgway remembers his father, Gary, as a relaxed man who never yelled and who took him camping, taught him to play baseball and tried to make him laugh. Even after his parents' divorce, Matthew stated that his father still played an active role in his life. Matthew's suffering began after the person he believed was a regular dad turned out to be responsible for the murder of forty-eight sex workers.

The Daughter Who Solved Her Father's Crimes

Let me introduce you to April Balascio. Her father is serial killer Edward Wayne Edwards, a handyman, father of five, and murderer of at least five women between 1977 and 1996; he is suspected of several more. Balascio describes her dad as both utterly charming and incredibly smart—and an abusive, compulsive liar with a terrible temper.

Ms. Balascio states that, even as a child, she knew something about her dad was wrong. He had once been on the FBIs Ten Most Wanted list for a robbery he committed. When she was in the second grade, he took her to a park where he "stumbled upon" two dead bodies. He had a strange habit of suddenly moving their family from town to town in the middle of the night. And she noticed he collected newspaper clippings of stories about certain murders.

But it wasn't until 2009, at age forty, that she started putting two and two together. She started by Googling cold cases from the various towns she'd grown up in, coming across two teens, Kelly Drew and Tim Hack, who, in 1980, had been murdered near a Sullivan, Wisconsin campground where Edwards worked as a handyman. Balascio talked to a detective who'd worked the case. A DNA test confirmed that Edwards was the teens' murderer. He ultimately confessed to several additional killings in Ohio, including two young women in Ohio and, in 1996, his twenty-four-year-old foster son. Edwards died in prison in 2011 while awaiting the death penalty.

94. How Could the Spouse of a Serial Killer Not Know What's Going On? When you look at later interviews with the spouses of serial killers, their reaction seems to be somewhere between denial and astonishment. Often, as we've already discussed, this is because the killer is so well-behaved in the bright light of day. The mask he wears hides any hint of the darkness that is apparent once he is arrested.

Sometimes, his behavior gives us a hint. Maybe he has unexplained periods away from home or an unusual number of miles logged on the family car. *Maybe* she wonders if her husband is having an affair. But who would suspect anything worse?

A few did find more direct—and damning—clues. John Wayne Gacy's wife found out that he had molested boys. Paula Rader, wife of Dennis Rader (the BTK murderer), accidentally found a poem he had written about killing his sixth victim; Rader told her it was for a college class course assignment. Robert Lee Yates' wife found a blood stain in the back of the car and discovered he had cut a hole in their attic so he could watch their neighbors having sex. Darcie Brudos, wife of serial killer Jerry Brudos, was not allowed to go into their attic or garage without first announcing herself on an intercom.

Odd behaviors? Yes. Disturbing behaviors? Definitely. But it's only with the benefit of hindsight that they singled out a serial killer.

Part 7: Victims, Crime Fighters, and the Ripple Effects of Crime.

Serial killers, on average, approach thirty-one potential victims before they get one under their control. Sometimes the situation isn't right; sometimes the predator is interrupted; sometimes the intended victim senses something and gets away. There is no guaranteed defense against a serial killer, but we may get a warning; when our intuition senses danger, we experience it as fear. Listen to it.

95. How Do Serial Killers Select Their Victims? This, of course, depends on the motive of the serial killer and the need(s) the violence is serving. Obviously, a black-widow serial killer is going to target her lovers or spouses; a revenge serial killer may strike back at the person whom he believes injured him or people this person loves, while a healthcare serial killer is going to kill his patients. This question most often arises when we are talking about sexually motivated serial killers, who *may* prefer a specific look or body type (for example, thin young women with long, blond hair).

The idea that serial killers wait for the perfect victim is somewhat overrated. It's true that some sexually motivated serial killers have a fantasy of an "ideal victim" based on race, gender, certain physical characteristics, or some other special quality. Gerald Gallego, for instance, would spend hours at a local mall trolling for who, to him, was the right victim. These preferences tend to evolve over time. At first, a serial killer's victim choice may seem almost random, or at least based on some extremely loose criteria (a woman, for example, or a teenage boy). As his killing career progresses, and he develops confidence in his ability to lure or kidnap a victim, some serial killers narrow down the type of victim they prefer and will stalk a more specific type of victim.

However, even those with distinct victim preferences will sometimes strike if the opportunity presents itself. Some serial killers are much more concerned with picking a victim who is vulnerable, such as a sex worker or homeless person, than in scouting out fantasy lookalikes. And some serial killers just aren't that picky; when the urge to kill comes on, his criteria is who is available and accessible.

I'm *Really* Killing My Mother

Ever since the 1960s movie *Psycho*, there have been a lot of myths about why serial killers target a particular victim. The most popular, of course, is that serial killers are seeking out victims who symbolically represent a woman in their life who had hurt them in some way—a girlfriend who'd dumped him or a mother who'd abandoned him. Mothers, especially, get a bad rap.

But that's not true. First of all, while we tend to think serial-killer victims are women, the statistics show us that relatively equal numbers of men (48.6 percent) and women (51.4 percent) are targeted by serial killers; when you take into account the fact that there are more women than men in the world, it practically evens out.

Neither are the victims carbon copies of someone the killer knows. It's true that a few serial killers have talked about a loose association between a past relationship and their murder victims; Ed Kemper, who targeted UC-Santa Cruz students, once said his victims didn't *look* like his mother but were the college kids she *admired* (his mother worked at the university). Kemper later admitted to longstanding homicidal fantasies about his highly critical, domineering mother and turned himself in after killing and decapitating her. James DeAngelo cried out "I hate you, Bonnie" during some of his rapes; it turns out his fiancé, Bonnie Colwell, had broken off their engagement years before.

More often than not, though, this symbolic link between a past trauma and current victim is murky. Here's an example. When I was growing up, Ted Bundy was thought to target young, attractive women with long dark hair parted in the middle. He struck fairly close to my house and it was chilling to me as a high school senior because I wore my hair in exactly the same way. There were even theories that he was choosing women who resembled a lost love who had dumped him and was psychologically killing her over and over again.

Ted, himself, however, scoffed at this and said that his only criteria for victims was that they were "reasonably attractive." It turns out that hundreds of thousands of young women wore their hair in the same way; it was the style at the time—and their hairstyle may have had nothing to do with the victims he chose.

96. How Do Serial Killers *Lure* Their Victims? Some serial killers are impulsively opportunistic. They take advantage of people in vulnerable situations—someone walking alone at dark or in an isolated area, a motorist who is stranded on the side of the road with a busted car, someone leaving a bar after having a little too much to drink. More than one simply walked around a neighborhood, looking for an unlocked door; if the house was secure, they simply shrugged their shoulders and moved on.

Other serial killers put in considerably more effort to find their victims. Some have disguised themselves as authority figures; Dennis Rader, the BTK killer who killed ten people between 1974 and 1991, posed as a telephone repairman with at least one victim and as a private investigator with another. Hillside Strangler Ken Bianchi would pose as a police officer and order victims into his cruiser. Charles William Davis, who killed up to five women in late 1975 through August 1976, used his police lieutenant father's resources to help him capture women he'd spotted while driving. He would follow his target in his car and, when the intended victim parked hers, he would run her license plate through his dad's system. He would then page her to tell her she had left her lights on and, when she returned, he would strike.

One of the most despicable ruses favored by several serial killers is to prey on the kindness of strangers. Ted Bundy often pretended to have a broken arm, luring kind young women to help him carry books back to his car. In the late 1980s, Scottish serial killer Robert Black pretended to have car trouble and attempted to snatch a 15-year-old when she stopped to offer assistance on a street near her home; luckily, she was able to fight him off and get away. Four young children between ages five and eleven were not so lucky; he kidnapped, raped, and murdered them after promising to show them kittens.

Stranger Danger for College Students

While parents often worry about strangers snatching young children, teenagers are actually the most frequent victims of both stranger and acquaintance kidnappings. Eighty percent of stranger-abductors are of children age twelve and older; seventy percent of these victims are girls. College-age women are also vulnerable; in 2013, seventy-two young adults—mainly women aged eighteen to twenty-five—were abducted by a stranger in the United States.

However, while the odds of any abduction are small, there is a psychological factor that can increase the vulnerability of teens and young adults; their sense of invincibility. As anyone who's parented a teen or young adult knows (and, like me, has likely passed many a sleepless night worrying about it), it's pretty common for young people to think they're bulletproof and immortal. I can certainly remember a few harrowing college experiences which, looking back, could be featured on a poster titled "Bad Judgment." It wasn't that I didn't think bad things couldn't happen; they just couldn't happen to *me*. Perhaps you can relate.

Here's how easily it could happen. In 2014, national investigative correspondent Jeff Rossen partnered with Hofstra University in an experiment to see how wary college students would be when interacting with a stranger. Posing as a reality-show casting director with a van and a home video, Rossen randomly invited college students to come into his van and audition for a new reality show.

Not only did half of the students willingly enter the van, many of them filled out a form containing all of their personal information (name, address, and phone number). A few even handed over a personal cellphone when Jeff Rossen asked to borrow it, leaving them completely unable to call for help if they really were in danger.

A similar 2006 study at Princeton and John Jay College of Justice found that about one in four of their college subjects fell for common lures used by predators (assisting an "injured" man carry and place books in a van, or agreeing to accompany a complete stranger on his trip downtown in exchange for cash). One young man even allowed his hands to be duct-taped behind his back after getting into a van when told he could be part of a reality show. Interestingly, almost all of the students who got in the van said they felt "weird" or "uncomfortable" about it—but did it anyway.

97. What is Life Like for the Family of a Missing Person?

There is a special kind of hell families live in when they don't know where a loved one is, but still hope that they will be found. We refer to this particularly dreadful dilemma as *ambiguous loss,* a grief with no explanation and no clear end in sight. Families in this predicament often describe feeling stuck, not wanting to give up hope but unable to grieve and move on.

They second guess everything, wondering if they could have done something to prevent their disappearance. They obsess over every possible scenario. Has she been kidnapped? Is he hurt somewhere and needs help? It's even harder if it's a missing child; as time passes, the family may wonder if they have forgotten them or been told the family abandoned him or her. Imagine how horrible that would be.

There is no easy answer for how to deal with this. Ultimately, each family has to battle through their pain and uncertainty and do so at their own pace. We, as mental health professionals, also struggle with how to help. How do we help them find a balance between unrealistic hope and bleak pessimism?

While it might seem that keeping hope alive would be better than giving up, studies of families of missing soldiers shows that might not always be the case. A recent study compared two groups of Bosnian and Herzegovinian women; one group were widows of soldiers killed during the 1992-95 war while the other women's husbands were still "missing." The women whose husbands' fates were unknown had higher levels of traumatic grief, depression, and suicidal thoughts. A similar study in Colombia, South America (looking at families of the "disappeared" versus confirmed dead) yielded similar results, also finding that the more strongly family members clung to hope, the more distressed they were.

Granted; there is a difference between a missing soldier or political activist and a family member who seems to disappear off the face of the earth. And I would never want to close the door on the idea that my missing child or mother or sister might be found. At the same time, being able to continue living life would seem to not only be a necessary survival strategy, but an honor to the lost family member. Perhaps that's why so much of the progress we've made with victim's rights and proactive policing have been spearheaded by family members, who've found a way not only to keep moving forward, but to protect others along the way.

Once-Missing Daughter Now Looks for Missing Mom

Imagine finding out that your adopted uncle was a serial killer who murdered your mom. That's what happened to Heather Tiffany Robinson who, at age fifteen, discovered that her birth name was Tiffany Lynn Stasi and that her biological mother, 19-year-old Lisa, had been murdered by John Robinson in 1985.

Nineteen-year old Lisa Stasi and baby Tiffany had last been seen in Chicago with John Robinson. Stasi had met Robinson (who introduced himself as John Osborne) while she was staying at a battered women's shelter in Kansas City, Kansas. She had left Tiffany's dad at the end of 1984 and was looking for ways to support herself and her young daughter. Robinson/Osborne encouraged Stasi to sign up for the Kansas City Outreach Program, an organization he allegedly founded to help young mothers get on their feet. He promised Stasi free room and board while she earned her GED. It was all a lie and, by mid-January 1985, Lisa Stasi was dead.

Around this time, John Robinson told his brother and sister-in-law, who had been trying to conceive for five years and were looking to adopt, that a young woman at a local Kansas City, Missouri Rodeway Inn had committed suicide and left behind a four-month old daughter who was available to them. Overjoyed, Donald and Frida Robinson welcomed the baby into their home and named her Heather.

Heather had always known she was adopted. But in 2000, following her uncle's 1999 arrest, she learned that her mother was one of eight women John Robinson killed. Lisa Stasi's relatives had long given up on finding the missing mother and child. Over the years, Heather gradually got to know her maternal grandmother, Pat Sylvester, who died in 2018. She has yet to meet her biological father. (He reached out to her when the story initially broke but Heather said she was not ready to meet him.)

But there is one person Heather is determined to find; her mother, Lisa. Stasi's remains have never been found and, so far, 75-year-old Robinson (who has been on death row since 2002) has refused to acknowledge the murder or provide information about the body. But Heather says she will never give up; it took fifteen years for her biological family to find her and she'll spend however long it takes until she finds her biological mom.

98. What Is Life Like for the Families of Known Victims?

Anyone who has listened to victim impact statements after a serial killer's trial has gotten a glimpse of the avalanche of emotions that surviving victims feel. They relive the terror, anger, and pain they experienced during the actual attack. They talk about the impact the crime has had on the rest of their lives—the lost innocence, the nightmares, the psychological devastation. Many also talk about their painful but victorious struggle to regain their personal power and speak out for other crime victims.

But one of the biggest secrets of serial murder is just how far the devastation spreads. Statistically speaking, each murder victim leaves behind seven to ten people who cared about him or her. These are secondary victims who not only have to grieve the loss of a loved one, but also come to terms with the horrible way they died. It's common for family members to obsessively think about revenge or have agonizing visions of their loved one's last hours. Many family members describe overwhelming feelings of guilt and helplessness over not protecting their loved one. Yolanda Robinson-Vann, whose mother, Fathyma, was murdered by serial killer, Phillip Jablonski, in 1991 (he also killed four other women between 1978 and 1991), says she is still haunted by the fact that she had dreams of her mother being murdered several months ahead of time and got bad vibes the one time she met her mother's killer.

Losing a loved one to violence brings some additional burdens. In the midst of their grief, family members typically have to deal with greater intrusion of the media and criminal justice systems, which can be traumatizing in and of themselves. This is especially true if the family member was in a vulnerable group such as sex workers or drug users, which have historically been stigmatized and judged. At a time when family members need support and comfort, they are all too often viewed with a jaundiced eye, and their dead sister, daughter, or mom boiled down to what she did instead of the complicated person she was.

But some families have transformed their grief into courage. In November, 2016, twenty-year-old college student Sarah Butler was murdered by serial killer Khalil Wheeler-Weaver after he convinced her to meet him through the social-media site Tagged. Her family and friends were directly responsible for his arrest.

Home for the Thanksgiving holidays, Sarah told her mother she was going to meet a friend and borrowed her car. No one ever saw her again. Frantic, her family and friends began searching. While looking for clues to her disappearance on Sarah's social media accounts, Sarah's sister and friend came across a man named Khalil Wheeler-Weaver's Tagged profile; the two had been communicating with each other shortly before Sarah disappeared. Suspicious, they created a fake profile, alerted police, and eventually arranged a meeting with Wheeler-Weaver at a Panera Bread in Glen Ridge, New Jersey, a small community approximately thirteen miles north of Newark Liberty International Airport. When he arrived, police were waiting for him and took him in for questioning. They also thought he was suspicious but, since Sarah had not been found, let him go.

Sadly, in early December, Sarah's body was found hidden underneath a pile of sticks and leaves on Eagle Rock Reservation in West Orange, New Jersey. Police then searched Wheeler-Weaver's home and found incriminating internet searches ("how to make homemade poisons to kill humans; what chemical can you put on a rag and hold to someone's face that will make them go to sleep immediately") and cell-phone tracks that placed him at three separate murder scenes. DNA matching Wheeler-Weaver's was also found underneath Sara Butler's fingernails. He was ultimately convicted of the murder of three women and attempted murder of a fourth. Without the Butler family's actions, it is likely Wheeler-Weaver would have continued to kill.

Crime Bills: The Lost Ones' Legacies

Amber Alerts. Chelsea's law. Polly Klaas' Three Strikes Law. The Adam Walsh Child and Safety Protection Act. The lives of all of these children for whom these laws were named were cut short by a predator.

But thousands of other children have been safer—and perhaps saved—because of them. Family members of murder victims have been responsible for pushing legislation through that, law by law, has tightened the loopholes through which serial predators have slipped; for instance, their activism has resulted in a faster police response when a child goes missing, better tracking of sex offenders, and increased sentences for violent offenders.

99. How Are Most Serial Killers Caught? It's pretty amazing to think that some of the most sophisticated serial killers get caught for the dumbest reasons. Among the lamest; a parking ticket (David Berkowitz), a stolen car (Ted Bundy), a dropped ID card (Peter Goebbels), or a blocked drain pipe (Dennis Nilsen). And while DNA, witness testimony, and fingerprints may be what eventually seals a serial killer's fate, it's often the serial killer's "mistakes" that draw attention to him in the first place. Here are some of the most common:

- **They stick to the familiar.** It's difficult to get away with one murder, much less a series of them. So, once they begin killing, many serial killers develop a routine that they stick to; they kill close to home or work, they dump bodies in the same area, and so forth. While this makes it easier for the killer, it also makes it easier for law enforcement, who can narrow down their search parameters and monitor sites where bodies have been found.
- **They underestimate their victims (and their families).** Many a serial killer has been undermined by a victim who has survived and helped police track him (or her) down. Also, perhaps because of their own lack of attachment to others, serial killers typically underestimate the love and relentless determination of family members to find a loved one who is missing or bring his or her killer to justice. Certain victims may raise the alarm sooner; a college student or family member is more likely to have a predictable routine and close regular contacts with friends and family than perhaps someone who is living on the streets or caught up in sex work or drug addiction. But few people have no one who would speak out if they disappeared.

Victims Who Got Away

Serial killers may be smart or devious or cunning, but they are not brave. Ever hear about a serial killer who chose his victim and gave her a 50/50 chance of getting away? Me neither. There's a reason why serial killers pick vulnerable victims and either lie and cheat their way into their victims' lives or ambush them when they least expect it; cowardice. It's the victims are the real unsung heroes when we talk about daring deeds and heart-stopping courage.

Here's just one example and her name is Heather Saul. "He pulled a gun on me! He was going to kill me!" Those are the chilling words caught in the background of a Charleston, South Carolina 911 call Heather made on July 18, 2015 after she faced off with an attacker who pointed a 9 mm gun at her chest and tried to rape her. She fought back so hard that her attacker, Neal Falls, lost control of his gun. Heather grabbed the weapon and blindly fired it, killing the 45-year-old Falls in self-defense. Heather, who met Falls after connecting via the escort section of Backpage.com, was not charged in the incident.

What police discovered in the trunk of Falls' car had state investigators wondering if Falls was responsible for other murders in various states. Falls had what police are calling a "kill kit," which included four sets of handcuffs, an ax, a machete, bulletproof vests, knives, a box cutter, a large container of bleach, and a large number of trash bags. Since his death, investigators have connected him to ten murders in Nevada and Ohio; they also found a list of six sex workers in Falls' pocket that they now believe he intended to kill after he disposed of Heather.

Heather is no unicorn. Victims have escaped from even the most notorious serial killers—Ted Bundy (Carol DaRonch), Alexander Pechuskin (Maria Viricheva), Richard Ramirez (Whitney Bennett), Robert Hansen (Cindy Paulson), etc. Some of them were lucky (in 2002, nineteen-year old and three months pregnant Maria Viricheva managed to survive being pushed down a well) while others survived by outsmarting or outmaneuvering their captor. In 1988, Teresa Thornhill fought off serial killer Robert Black on the side of the road; in 1986, Kate Moir (kidnapped by Australian serial killers David and Catherine Birnie) escaped through a window after being tortured, raped, and handcuffed. And, in 2018, Erika Pena jumped out of a car with her shirt torn off and a gun pointed at her, which led to the capture of serial killer and Border Patrol agent Juan David Ortiz. Each of these women played a pivotal role in her perpetrator's conviction, undoubtedly saving the lives of other women.

• **They put their psychological needs before safety.** Some (but not most) serial killers have a need for attention; this is also true of other criminals. They taunt the police; they toy with the media. A small minority (around three percent) actually insert themselves into investigations; in one case, a murderer actually went back to the scene of the crime after it had been processed and left new evidence (clothes the victim had been wearing on the day she died). They know it's risky but they just can't help it; their narcissism demands some degree of recognition for their "accomplishments." And what better way to feed your sense of superiority than hiding from police in plain sight?

Not surprisingly, this ploy often backfires. Not only does it up the ante in terms of police pressure, writings and phone calls have helped police link crimes together or alerted them to crimes they were unaware of. Think how easy it might be, if you're part of a volunteer search party for a missing person whom you've actually murdered, to let a detail slip out that only the killer would know, or how tempting it would be to make sure you're the one who actually finds the body. Sure, it might be thrilling to show the media what a criminal genius you are or thumb your nose at cops. But, in the long run, if you're trying to avoid justice, too much attention is a bad thing.

Along these same lines, some serial killers feel psychologically compelled to revisit the crime scene. The majority of them don't; however, while we don't have statistics, empirical evidence does suggest that, as a group, serial killers (and arsonists) are more likely to do it than other types of offenders. Going back to the crime scene keeps the fantasy alive and helps them relive what they have done.

But while returning to the scene of the crime might prolong a serial killer's enjoyment, it also increases the odds that physical evidence will be left behind or that they will be spotted by cops staking out the area. Serial killers Arthur Shawcross and Gary Ridgway gambled on a trip down memory lane and lost—both were arrested when returning to the scene of the crime. (Ironically, it was Ted Bundy's advice to law enforcement to stake out gravesites of recent Green River victims that eventually led to Ridgway's capture.)

• **They underestimate the weapons against them.** Serial killers often have a hard time keeping up with the latest forensic technology—the latest in DNA advancements, the power of cell signals, the ability to recover erased computer data, or the access that law enforcement has to databases. They also downplay how much evidence a body holds onto; every time a victim's body is found, it tells a story about the predator who left it there.

The Fake Serial-Killer Expert

Catching serial killers is tough enough without one of the "good guys" turning out to be a pathological liar. In 2020, famous French serial-killer expert Stephane Bourgoin confessed that his world-famous crime-fighting career was founded on lies. Before he was outed, the 67-year-old Bourgoin had written more than seventy-five books, testified in numerous criminal cases, and was a guest lecturer for trainees at the French national judiciary police academy. It was all a lie.

His downfall began with a series of anonymous YouTube videos accusing Bourgoin of deception. This sparked a more formal investigation and exposed plagiarized books and fabrications (he falsely claimed for example, that his wife had been murdered and that he had once interviewed Charles Manson). In reality, the murdered woman was a bartender he knew casually and he never laid eyes on the infamous cult leader.

Bourgoin is now profusely apologetic, claiming his guilt over not telling the truth had weighed heavily on him. The evidence suggests otherwise; like many of the killers he profiled, he did not come clean until his back was against the wall. Another thing Bourgoin apparently has in common with his serial-killing subjects is the refusal to take responsibility for his actions. In an interview with a French newspaper shortly after he was exposed, he blamed his "exaggerations" on the fact that he "always had the deep feeling of not being 'really loved.'"

100. Has anyone ever been convicted of a murder that was actually committed by a serial killer? Yes, and it's happened more than once. When we don't usually think of it, the victims of serial killers also include innocent people who are rotting in prison, convicted of the murders the real culprit committed.

Teenagers Rhonda Johnson and Sharon Shaw disappeared in August 1971 while at a beach in Galveston, Texas; their remains were found in January 1972. Michael Lloyd Self, a local sex offender, confessed but always insisted that police officers forced him to do so at gunpoint. No one believed him and, in 1975, he was convicted and sentenced to life in prison.

In 1976, two of the officers who heard his "confession" were arrested for numerous bank robberies and received sentences of thirty to fifty years, giving some merit to Self's claim that his interrogators had skirted the law. In 1998, Edward Harold Bell, a convicted serial killer, admitted to the murders of Johnson and Shaw but, before he was exonerated, Self died from cancer in prison.

Here's another example. In March 2004, David Allen Jones was released from prison after DNA proved that he did not commit any of the three separate murders for which he had been convicted. Between September and December 1992, the bodies of four women believed to be sex workers were found—strangled—near an elementary school in Los Angeles. Around this same time—December 1992—Jones was arrested for the rape of a woman who had a record of prostitution; she had identified him in a photo lineup.

Once he was in custody, Jones was asked about the string of murders of sex workers that had occurred over the previous three months. This apparently became the focus of their questioning. After being taken to each crime scene and vigorously questioned, Jones, who had an IQ of 62 and whose blood type did not match the serology in the deceased victims' rape kits, confessed and was eventually convicted. Fortunately, California's new post-conviction DNA statute resulted in Jones' DNA being compared to the DNA found on two of the murdered women. The resulting profile matched that of a serial murderer already in prison for attacking women in the Los Angeles area—Chester Turner. Turner was subsequently charged with ten additional murders.

Some people might argue that these two men were certainly not model citizens and if someone who was already guilty of other violent crimes gets fingered for additional ones, well, that's something we shouldn't lose much sleep over. Not only is this not the way our justice system is supposed to work, but consider this: data from the National Registry of Exonerations shows that there have been sixty-two serial killers who killed one hundred and fourteen additional victims after an innocent person was incarcerated for his initial crimes. These victims could have been saved had the real perpetrator been arrested earlier in the killing career.

Framed for a Serial Killer's Crime

On January 23, 1990, twenty-three-year old Taunja Bennett was brutally raped and murdered in Portland, Oregon. One of the many locals who read about it in the news was fifty-seven-year old Laverne Pavlinac. Pavlinac was apparently somewhat of a true crime buff who was familiar with police procedures, closely followed crime reports in the newspapers, and was a dedicated watcher of the detective television show *Matlock*. She was also an abused woman looking for a way out of her ten-year relationship with thirty-nine-year old John Sosnoske.

For some reason, Pavlinac decided this case was her ticket. She did her homework, researching as many details about the crimes as possible. She found out which detectives were investigating, contacted them and blamed Sosnoske. She then contacted them and told them that her boyfriend had committed the rape and murder. Pavlinac first told police that Sosnoske had bragged about the murder; no one listened. When that didn't move the case forward, Pavlinac began to up the ante. Over time, she made increasingly incriminating statements, not only about Sosnoske but about her own role in the murder.

She wound up claiming Sosnoske had forced her to act as his accomplice. She said she had been with her boyfriend the night he met Ms. Bennet at a bar, had personally witnessed the sexual assault, and had unwillingly held a rope around Bennett's neck as Sosnoske strangled her. With investigators in tow, she was able to pinpoint the approximate location of the body (likely either from newspaper details or hints given by the investigating detectives) and, a search of their home turned up a piece of paper with the words "T. Bennett – a good piece" on it. A piece of torn-off blue jean material was also found (part of Bennett's blue jeans had been missing when she was found but this piece found at Pavlinac's place did not match the victim's clothing). Sosnoske himself, an alcoholic who suffered from blackouts, seemed to half-believe the story himself.

Interestingly, this was not the first time Pavlinac had made false allegations against her significant other; Pavlinac's daughter later claimed that her mother was so desperate to get rid of her abusive live-in boyfriend she had tried to turn Sosnoske in for a bank robbery a year earlier but the FBI "saw through her story that time."

It does not appear that Pavlinac intended for Sosnoske to be in prison for life. One of Sosnoske's appellate lawyers stated that Pavlinac had thought she would implicate Sosnoske, he would get arrested, she would be rid of him, and then she would confess to having falsely accused him. He would be released from jail and they both would be free. Unfortunately, Pavlinac soon realized that some bells cannot be un-rung.

Sosnoske was arrested for first-degree murder and Pavlinac charged as an accessory. During her trial, Pavlinac recanted her story to a jury with deaf ears; she was easily convicted and sentenced to ten years. Sosnoske, whose trial had not started and was terrified he might get the death penalty if convicted, pleaded no contest and was sentenced to life. Fortunately, both were released after four years when serial killer Keith Hunter Jesperson confessed and was convicted of eight murders, including Bennett's.

Jesperson himself played a key role in Pavlinac's and Sosnoske's releases, taking a polygraph and giving specific information about Bennett's murder that helped free the imprisoned innocents. It would be nice to think Jesperson's motive was altruistic, but the evidence suggests that his motivations were to avoid extradition to Wyoming for another murder he had committed, where he was likely to face the death penalty, as well as his ire over the possibility of not getting "credit" for Bennett's murder. After all, for years he had been bragging about his murders on truck stop bathroom stalls and in letters to the media and police, all signed with his "happy face" signature.

101. What Are the Best Ways to Escape a Serial Killer?
A German criminologist and former police commissioner, Stephan Harbort, actually tried to figure this out. He studied one hundred and fifty-five serial killers and their six hundred and seventy-four individual crimes between 1945 and 1995, interviewing many of the murderers and one hundred and seven of their surviving victims, to see why some victims survived when so many others died. He published his findings in 2001.

One of his strongest (and scariest) findings was how drastically the odds of survival went down once a serial killer actually had the victim under his control; only 15.9 percent of the victims survived under these circumstances. In other words, the odds of getting away from a serial murderer typically happen *before* you get in his car or go to his house. This suggests that no matter how tempting it might be to comply if someone points a gun at you and tells you to go with them or be shot, you might actually be better off, statistically, taking your chances screaming and running in a zigzag than avoiding the immediate danger and hoping for a later escape.

Of those who *were* captive, forty-three percent of the surviving victims escaped because the injuries weren't fatal, thirty-six percent because the victim fought back physically or verbally, fifteen percent because the killer thought the victim was dead and left, 15 percent because a third person scared the murderer away, 8.4 percent because the victim found a chance to flee, and 4.7 percent because the victim outwitted the killer (for example, one woman mentioned that her friend had written down his license-plate number, while another engaged the killer in such intimate conversation that she became a "real person" to him and he said he felt he had to let her go). So about half survived due to sheer luck and about half took advantage of an opportunity to change their fate. It's important to remember that those opportunities (a chance to run, an opportunity to fight back) that helped survivors aren't available to every victim.

It's also important to note that fighting back was not without its risks. Self-defense only worked if it was all-out and extreme. Mild resistance not only didn't help (73.3 percent) but made things worse; the serial killer became more violent. Massive resistance—an all-out fight—also led to more violence, but sometimes it paid off; 17.6 percent of the victims were able to escape. However, this isn't always the best strategy; in Harbort's interviews with the serial killers themselves, a few of them said they let some of their victims go *because* they were submissive, insisting the survivors would have killed them if they'd fought back. Harbort concluded that once a serial killer has someone in his or her clutches, the victim's best strategy is often determined by the killer's personality and the victim's best bet is to follow his or her intuition—something that's always worth paying attention to.

Conclusion

So, what do you think now that we're at the end of our journey together? How you do feel about serial killers; are they less interesting or more fascinating? Are the good guys winning or the bad guys becoming more sophisticated? And what do you think about all of the true-crime podcasts and television shows?

I, of course, have some opinions about these questions myself. For better or worse, I will probably always be intrigued by the extremes of human behavior, especially the dark ones. I think it's in my nature. What I ask of myself is that I use it for good, whether I'm evaluating a violent offender up for parole, testifying at a trial, assisting on a cold-case investigation, or talking about it with the general public. I cannot forget the suffering of victims and their families; I've worked with enough to witness the devastation firsthand.

Are we winning the war against violent crime? Well, we've sure won some battles. Violent crime rates are down by more than fifty percent in comparison to the 1990s, the number of serial killers has dropped, and we have some new weapons to help us.

But most Americans think violent crime, including serial murder, is *up*. We're a lot more aware of the bad things that can happen, i.e., who would hitchhike these days, leave their doors unlocked or let their kids play unsupervised after dark? Kids grow up more fearful than they used to, but also safer.

Progress, though, is rarely linear. Mass murder is up. Rape has been increasing. And, while overall murder rates have decreased, so have solve rates; today, the national clearance rate for murder is around sixty percent. In 1965, it was over ninety percent. So, fewer people get murdered and fewer murders get solved. And we don't know what percentage of these unsolved murders *could* be the work of a serial offender.

For forensic psychologists like me, we're still trying to find that recipe that makes a serial killer so we can remove or change the ingredients. We still don't have it. But we do know some of the most common elements: trauma, abuse, social isolation, genetic vulnerabilities, a head injury. There are a lot of crime-fighting ploys we can use before someone ever breaks the law: stamping out child abuse, getting troubled kids into treatment sooner, adding social and emotional skills (like anger management and managing your emotions) to school curriculums, teach verbal and self-defense strategies as part of physical education, strengthen bonds between communities and law enforcement. I am convinced that each of these would, in some way, reduce the odds an at-risk child becomes a deadly predator.

As far as all the recent hype about serial killers and true crime, there no doubt have been a few shows whose portrayal of a serial killer has bordered on the glamorous. There are a few podcasts in which the tone suggests the host has forgotten that the victims are real people. There have been a few instances where armchair detectives have intruded into the privacy of a grieving family or where people have withheld valuable information from law enforcement in an attempt to get credit for solving the case. Let's make sure these things stop.

But think of all the good that's been done. True-crime fans and armchair detectives have called in vital tips, identified murder suspects, and found (or identified) missing loved ones. In 1968, true crime fan Todd Mathews' father-in-law found the dead body of a young woman; no one knew who she was. Twenty years later, Mathews single-handedly identified her as Barbara Ann Hackman Taylor after spending hours searching through missing-persons records. In 2016, journalist Billy Jensen posted surveillance footage of a murder on a social media ad; tips poured in and the perpetrator was arrested and convicted. And on and on.

I am proud of the fact that more of us are speaking up when we see something that's wrong and taking steps to help make it right. I love the involvement, energy, dedication, and advocacy that drives many internet sleuths to spend hours doing everything from advocating for better tracking of missing persons to pouring over cold cases.

Clearly, there are some guidelines and boundaries that need to be established and respected. We have some kinks to work out. But, overall, I think engagement is a good thing. Let us never forget what Irish statesmen and philosopher Edmund Burke said, "The only thing necessary for the triumph of evil is for good men [and women] to do nothing."

References

Aamodt, M. G. (2016, September 4). Serial killer statistics. Retrieved November 15, 2020, from http://maamodt.asp.radford.edu/serial killer information center/projectdescription.htm

Abe, K. (2020). Family Environment Decides Motives of Serial Killers. , (2), 46-48.

Adelstein, D., Diaz, E., Hood, M., McAuliffe, C., Pickett, T., Rule, M., & Tuason, T. (2020, April 8). Serial Killers & childhood Trauma. [Conference presentation]. SOARS 2020, University of North Florida, United States.

https://digitalcommons.unf.edu/cgi/viewcontent.cgi?article=1077&context=soars

Allely, C. S., Minnis, H., Thompson, L., Wilson, P., & Gillberg, C. (2014). Neurodevelopmental and psychosocial risk factors in serial killers and mass murderers. (3), 288–301. doi.org/10.1016/j.avb.2014.04.004

Appellee, v. Martha L. Woods, 484 F.2d 127 (1973). https://law.justia.com/cases/federal/appellate-courts/F2/484/127/195191/

Barker, T (2020). . Palgrave Macmillan.

Brummelman, E., Thomaes, S., Nelemans, S. A., Orobio de Castro, B., & Bushman, B. J. (2015). My child is God's gift to humanity: Development and validation of the Parental Overvaluation

Scale (POS). (4), 665–679. doi.org/10.1037/pspp0000012

Cauffiel, L. (2014). Forever and Five Days: The Chilling True Story of Love, Betrayal, and Serial Murder in Grand Rapids, Michigan. Mysterious Press: Open Road Media

Davies, K., & Woodhams, J. (2019). The Practice of Crime Linkage: A Review of the Literature. , (3), 169-200. doi: org/10.1002/jip.1531

Fairchild, G., Hawes, D. J., Frick, P. J., Copeland, W. E., Odgers, C. L., Franke, B., Freitag, C. M., & De Brito, S. A. (2019). Conduct disorder. (1), 43. https://doi.org/10.1038/s41572-019-0095-y

Farrell, A., Keppel, R., & Titterington, V. B. (2013). Testing Existing Classifications of Serial Murder Considering Gender: An Exploratory Analysis of Solo Female Serial Murderers. (3), 268-288.

Farrell, M. (2020). . London: Palgrave Macmillan.

Federal Bureau of Investigation. (2005). Serial murder. Retrieved November 15, 2020, from https://www.fbi.gov/stats-services/publications/serial-murder#epi

Fischer, C. A., Beckson, M., & Dietz, P. (2017). Factitious Disorder in a Patient Claiming to be a Sexually Sadistic Serial Killer. (3), 822-826.

Foubert, J. D., Clark-Taylor, A., & Wall, A. F. (2020). Is Campus Rape Primarily a Serial or One-Time Problem? Evidence from a Multicampus Study , (3-4), 296–311. doi.org/10.1177/1077801219833820

Fox, J. A., & DeLateur, M. J. (2014). Mass Shootings in America: Moving Beyond Newtown. , (1), 125–145. doi.org/10.1177/1088767913510297

Harbers, E., Deslauriers-Varin, N., Beauregard, E., & van der Kemp, J. J. (2012). Testing the Behavioral and Environmental Consistency of Serial Sex Offenders: A Signature Approach. , (3), 259-273.

Harbort, S. (2008). Düsseldorf: Droste Verlag.

Harrison, M. A., Hughes, S. M., & Gott, A. J. (2019). Sex differences in serial killers. 4), 295–310. https://doi.org/10.1037/ebs0000157

Harrison, M., Murphy, E., Ho, L. Y., Bowers, T., & Flaherty, C. (2015). Female serial killers in the United States: means, motives, and makings. (3),383 - 406. doi: 10.1080/14789949.2015.1007516

Harrison, M., & Frederick, E. J. (2020). Interested in serial killers? Morbid curiosity in college students. , 1-10.

Hickey, E. W. (2003). Encyclopedia of Murder and Violent Crime. London: Sage Publications.

Horan, L., & Beauregard, E. (2017). Pathways in the Offending Process of Sex Offenders who Target Marginalised Victims. , (3), 213-226.

Igo, N., & Beaman, J. (2020). Gender differences in serial homicide. Poster session presented at Oklahoma State University Center for Health Sciences Research Day 2020, Tulsa, United States. Retrieved from https://shareok.org/handle/11244/324207

Martin, E., Schwarting, D. E., & Chase, R. J. (2020, June). Serial Killer Connections Through Cold Cases. , Retrieved from https://nij.ojp.gov/library/publications/serial-killer-connections-through-cold-cases

Marono, A. J., Reid, S., Yaksic, E., & Keatley, D. A. (2020). A Behaviour Sequence Analysis of Serial Killers' Lives: From Childhood Abuse to Methods of Murder. , 1), 126–137. doi.org/10.1080/13218719.2019.1695517

Myers, W. C., Gooch, E., & Meloy, J. R. (2005). The role of psychopathy and sexuality in a female serial killer. , (3), 652–657.

Parfitt, C. H., & Alleyne, E. (2020). Not the Sum of Its Parts: A Critical Review of the MacDonald Triad. (2), 300–310. doi.org/10.1177/1524838018764164

Penn S. (2019, March 20). Psychology may help explain why male and female serial killers differ. ScienceDaily. Retrieved November 14, 2020 from www.sciencedaily.com/releases/2019/03/190320110622.htm

People v. Rutterschmidt, B209568 (2019). https://caselaw.findlaw.com/ca-court-of-appeal/1267298.html

People v. Jablonski, Docket # S041630, State of California (2006). https://scocal.stanford.edu/opinion/people-v-jablonski-33578

Proulx, J., Jonathan, J., & Higgs, T. (2020). Sexual Murderers. In Proulx, J., Cortoni, J., Jonathan, C., Leam A., & Letourneau, E. J. (Eds.), , (pp. 295-310). John Wiley and Sons Ltd.

Ramsland, K. M. (2007). . Praeger Publishers.

Raymond, S., Léger, A., & Gasman, I. (2019). The Psychopathological Profile of Cannibalism: A Review of Five Cases. , (5), 1568-1573.

Silvio, H., McCloskey, K., & Ramos-Grenier, J. (2007). Exploring the Phenomenon of Female Sexual Predator Serial Killers in the United States.

In Froeling, K. T (Eds.), (pp. 97-118). Nova Publishers.

Simkin, M. V., & Roychowdhury, V. (2018). Statistical study of time intervals between murders for serial killers. arXiv: Physics and Society.

The Federal Bureau of Investigation. (1999). Columbine High School. Retrieved November 15, 2020 from

https://vault.fbi.gov/Columbine%20High%20School%20/Columbine%20High%20School%20Part%201%20of%204/view

The Lust Murders. (1980). FBI Law Enforcement Bulletin. 4th Issue. United States. Public Affairs Office. https://www.ncjrs.gov/pdffiles1/Digitization/68689NCJRS.pdf

Vronsky, P. (2007). . New York, USA: Penguin Group.

Watts, A. L., Rohr, J. C., McCauley, K. L., Smith, S. F., Howe, K. L., & Lindfield, S. O. (2018). Do Psychopathic Birds of a Feather Flock Together? Psychopathic Personality Traits and Romantic Preferences, (2), 341-362.

Williams, D. (2017). Entering the Minds of Serial Murderers: The Application of Forensic Leisure Science to Homicide Research. (4), 376 - 383.

Williams, D. (2017). Mephitic projects: a forensic leisure science analysis of the BTK serial murders. , 2 (1), 24-37.

Williams, D. J., Thomas, J. N., & Arntfield, M. (2017). An Empirical Exploration of Leisure-Related Themes and Potential Constraints across Descriptions of Serial Homicide Cases. , (1), 69-84, doi: 10.1080/01490400.2017.1384941

Williamson, J. A. (2020). A Validation of Keppel and Walter's classification model for serial sexual murders (Publication No. 27964768) [Doctoral dissertation, Capella University]. ProQuest Dissertations Publishing.

Winston-Salem Journal. (2014, October 8). . https://journalnow.com/news/crime/algarad-forensic-psychiatric-evaluation/pdf_d4f50e06-4f50-11e4-aae4-001a4bcf6878.html

Woster, M. (2020). Differences in Characteristics of Criminal Behavior Between Solo and Team Killers (Publication No. 463) [Doctoral dissertation, National Louis University]. Retrieved from https://digitalcommons.nl.edu/diss/463

Yaksic, E., Allred, T. B., Drakulic, C., Mooney, R., De Silva, R., Geyer, P., Wills, A., Comerford, C., & Ranger, R. (2020) How much damage do serial homicide offenders wrought while the innocent rot in prison? A tabulation of preventable deaths as outcomes of sentinel events, . doi: 10.1080/1068316X.2020.1774590

Yorker, B. C. (2018, May 27). Expert Review for the Public Inquiry into the Safety and Security of Residents in the Long-term Care Homes System. http://longtermcareinquiry.ca/wp-content/uploads/Exhibit-163_Expert-Report-of-Professor-Beatrice-Crofts-Yorker.pdf

For More News About Joni Johnston,
Signup For Our Newsletter:
http://wbp.bz/newsletter

Word-of-mouth is critical to an author's long-term success. If you appreciated this book please leave a review on the Amazon sales page:
http://wbp.bz/serialkillersa

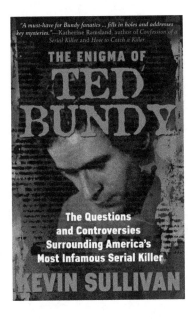

CPSIA information can be obtained
at www.ICGtesting.com
Printed in the USA
LVHW082048290321
682865LV00005B/16

9 781952 225512